COOKING

WITH

FRUIT

Cooking With Fruit

Ursula Grüniger

Translated from the German by L. Steinhart

Illustrations by Anne Knight

Mayflower

Granada Publishing Limited
Published in 1974 by Mayflower Books Ltd
Frogmore, St Albans, Herts AL2 2NF

First published in Great Britain 1971
This translation © George Allen & Unwin Ltd 1971
Made and printed in Great Britain by
Richard Clay (The Chaucer Press) Ltd, Bungay, Suffolk

'Cooking is a creative art'

For Gabriele and Eleonore

Foreword

'Children's liking for fruit is proof of its exceptional value, and they will retain it throughout life unless led astray by a faulty diet.'

Sebastian Kneipp

Dear Friend,

'To maintain good health and vigour is possible only if the body's needs for all the essential nutriments are met in full.' This statement by the German Society for Nutrition means that we need a diet which is light in terms of calories, one that does not burden the digestive organs nor strain the body; in short, we need plenty of vegetables and fruit.

Our grandmothers necessarily had to produce heavy meals and rich stews and soups to enable our grandfathers to carry out hard physical labour! We, however, who have machines to do the heavy work for us, have no need to stoke up with meals over-rich in calories; and, for the figure-conscious, a low-calorie mixed diet of lean meat, milk, cheese and fish with plenty of fruit and vegetables, is an absolute necessity. Moreover, we know that our food contains not only fats, carbohydrates, proteins, water and mineral salts, but also vitamins which, we realize, form an essential part of a complete diet; it is this realization which has led us to accept fruit as an indispensable ingredient in our diet.

Vitamin deficiencies lower the body's resistance to disease and can gravely impair our health. Vitamin C is essential in the diet of growing children for the building up and normal functioning of all body organs and for the strengthening of defences against colds. Fresh fruit is important for expectant mothers and nursing mothers and, if taken regularly, also prevents rheumatism, lumbago and gout in later life. In short, fruit forms an indispensable part of our diet in both sickness and health.

In this book I have suggested dishes containing fruit as an essential ingredient for every meal of the day and for every season of the year, not forgetting suitable dishes for the sick-room as well. In considering the numerous ways in which fruit can be used in the kitchen I have not restricted myself to German recipes only, but have taken many a peep into the cooking pots of other countries. Even the most imaginative cook sometimes feels that she is running out of new ideas so that an occasional foray into the repertories of foreign cooks helps prevent staleness.

Your family will derive great benefit from the inclusion of fruit dishes daily in your menus for, whether fresh from the market or out of the deep freeze, fruit remains invaluable as a part of our diet. Just one reminder: fruit, if eaten raw, must be ripe and should be washed before consumption. For the rest, you can allow your imagination free play, from the basic preparation in the kitchen to the final presentation of your dishes.

I hope you will enjoy it from start to finish.

Sincerely yours,
Ursula Grüniger

Contents

Introduction

FRUIT IN LEGEND AND HISTORY

Few of us, when faced with a colourful display of many kinds of fruit on a market stall or an alluring centrepiece on a festive table, will stop to consider the history or countries of origin of the various types of fruit presented to us; we simply take them for granted. Yet few of them are indigenous to Europe or have been known here from the beginning of recorded history.

The *apple* is one of Germany's oldest known fruits, enjoyed, according to legend, by the ancient Germanic gods in Valhalla. Apples originated in faraway Armenia. For the ancient Greeks the apple, like the vine, was the gift of Dionysus, and Pliny lists twenty-one different kinds. At the time of Charlemagne only four or five kinds were known in Germany, yet the number had grown to 200 in 1650. Today no fewer than 1,500 varieties are known.

Even if apples were no longer grown on our earth we would still be familiar with them through history and legend: the Tree of Knowledge in Paradise was an apple tree; and an apple was offered by Paris to Aphrodite, thus becoming the direct cause of the Trojan War. In earlier times, apples were regarded as precious and the Imperial apple, golden symbol of sovereign rule, was placed in the right hand of German emperors at their coronation.

The *Pear* is mentioned in the Odyssey. Regarded as the

sister of the apple, yet considered gentler, subtler and more delicate, as befitting its sex, this fruit was introduced from Western Asia by the ancient Greeks, who began its cultivation.

Cherries, both the sweet and Morello varieties, derive from Western Asia, and are called after the Greek-named town Kerasous in Pontus, Asia Minor. But even before recorded history the sweet variety had made its way to Europe. We find the lake dwellers of early Bronze Age Switzerland enjoying juicy cherries, long before the great Lucullus introduced the famous cherries of Pontus into Rome in 64 B.C. This particular newcomer to Roman orchards quickly spread to other parts of Europe.

Little is known about the history of *plums, switzens, mirabelles*, etc., and it is not clear which of these delectable varieties arrived on the scene first, although one branch is known to have come from Syria. Switzens, comparative newcomers to British fruit stalls, differ mainly by their slim shape from their more rounded plum cousins.

The *apricot* comes from Armenia and was brought to Greece in about A.D. 50. It was popular in Rome in Pliny's time, and appeared in Germany for the first time in 1565 in the ducal orchard at Stuttgart.

The *peach*, known to the Romans as the 'Persian apple', was introduced into Greece from Persia by Alexander the Great. The tree, however, came originally from China where it had been grown for 4,000 years and accorded religious honours.

Soft fruits have been valued for culinary and medicinal purposes both in Asia and in Europe for centuries. The *redcurrant*, known as 'St John's berry' in Germany because it ripens on that saint's day, has been popular since medieval times. The *blackcurrant* was discovered towards the end of the sixteenth century; its somewhat astringent bouquet and flavour has caused it to be less popular as a fresh fruit. However, its sugar and vitamin C contents are particularly high, and its juice makes a health-giving and enjoyable drink for all. *Gooseberries* have been cultivated since the eighteenth century. *Raspberries* and *blackberries* have been growing wild in our forests from time immemorial, and the gathering of berries has been both pastime and necessity for countless generations.

In the Middle Ages people began to cultivate some strains in their gardens. *Bilberries* and *cranberries* are still wild-growing berries, the latter growing at considerable altitudes in the Alps and other European mountains. Our commercially grown *strawberries* have been derived from the crossing of wild strawberries with strains from the Himalayas, Virginia and Chile; three continents thus have combined to produce this luscious fruit. Strangely enough, the strawberry was unknown to the Greeks and Romans and only found its way to Europe via North Africa and Spain in the Middle Ages. Today 400 varieties with various names are known to breeders.

The vine, with its *grape*, also found its way to Europe from the east, presumably from the river valleys of Asia. It is one of the oldest cultivated plants and was known to the ancient Syrians and Egyptians before 3500 B.C. Pliny relates that the Gauls grew several kinds of grapes in the first century of imperial Rome. Charlemagne, in the legends surrounding him, is praised as the patron of the vine.

Grapes are particularly rich in sugar and minerals and they should be brought to our dining tables frequently between August and December, the principal season. Grape juice is an aid in convalescence and there are medical centres in Merano, in the South Tyrol, where grape cures can be taken. Grape juice speeds up the metabolism, aids digestion, purifies the blood and is an aid to slimming. Do not, however, embark on a grape cure without consulting a doctor first.

A glass of red wine into which an egg yolk and a little sugar has been stirred is a tonic which was already known to our grandparents. The Americans like chilled grape juice as a morning cup and as a starter before meals. So do I, and it increases my feeling of wellbeing. One can always learn from others.

The *quince* came to us via Persia from the East. It was known in Greece in Homer's time and history tells us that it was sacred to Aphrodite, the goddess of love. Plutarch tells us that, on their wedding night, newly married couples had to eat a quince before entering the bridal chamber to give sweetness to their breath. Such strange customs as this partly survive to this day, for Greek brides still carry a golden apple (of the

13

Hesperides) when entering their husband's house for the first time. This use of the apple (quince) represents a symbolic dedication to Aphrodite. In Germany it was Charlemagne who ordered quinces to be planted. Quinces are exquisitely scented and the aroma which fills house and kitchen when quince jelly is made, is quite out of this world.

Finally, a few notes about the fruits imported from sunny lands which form an indispensable part of our diet, especially in winter.

Let us begin with the *lemon*, ancestor of all the citrus fruits. The soldiers of Alexander the Great's armies, fighting in Asia, noticed the yellow fruit among the dark green leaves; finding the juice enjoyable, they took cuttings of the trees home to Greece. Then the Arabs took up the cultivation of lemons and began to use it for medicinal purposes. Lemons are said to have been effective sometimes in preventing outbreaks of the plague during the Middle Ages.

Lemon trees bear fruit three times a year and each harvest has a different name. The fruits of the first blossoming are called primofiori. While this harvest is still in progress, a second crop ripens on the same trees and these bear the name limoni. Finally the tree is left without water for 4–5 weeks under the hot August sun. When the leaves begin to drop the trees are drenched with water; this process causes a third cycle of flower and fruit. These lemons reach the market still green and are sold under the name verdelli.

Lemons have become quite indispensable in modern cooking, as so many dishes, cakes and pastries acquire a more subtle and delicious flavour through the addition of lemon juice or rind (a word of warning here however – lemon skins are sometimes treated with diphenyl). Lemon juice is also deliciously refreshing and, as a hot drink, is a valuable aid in the sickroom.

China is the original home of the *orange*, the 'golden apple', which was brought to Europe by the Portuguese in the sixteenth century where it quickly conquered the coasts of the Mediterranean. Known for a long time under the name 'Chinese apple', the *orange*, rich in vitamin C, helps us over the 'end of winter' lassitude. It also contains valuable acids and vitamins

14

A (which gives you brighter eyes), B1 and B2. Breeders have produced a great number of different strains, such as pipless and 'blood' oranges, mandarins, the pipless clementine, etc.

The original home of the *grapefruit* is the Sunda Islands, where individual fruits are said sometimes to reach the size of a baby's head. We have to be content with somewhat smaller specimens.

The *pineapple* is the queen of all the fruits of sunnier climates. The claim is sometimes made that the sweetness of honey, the flavour of the strawberry, the bouquet of wine and the scent of the peach, are contained in it. Columbus discovered it in the West Indies where it is called 'nan meant' by the natives; from this the German and French name 'ananas' is probably derived. Pineapples, both fresh and tinned, are imported to Europe mostly from Hawaii. It is a highly popular fruit. Many salads would be incomplete without it, and even a dish of sauerkraut is improved by its subtle flavour.

The *banana* is another tropical fruit. Some say that it was first discovered in the forests of the Himalayas. Humboldt, however, reports that it was already known to the Incas and Aztecs. Be that as it may, it forms an important part in the diets of babies and young children. It is as easily digested (it takes $2\frac{1}{2}$ hours to digest an apple as compared with $1\frac{3}{4}$ hours for a banana) as it is versatile, and we shall see that it can be used, not only as a dessert, but also in salads, as a vegetable and as an accompaniment to meat and rice dishes.

But enough for now; fruit is a fascinating subject and when next you place a bowl filled with many varieties on your table you can truthfully claim that it contains a chapter of world history.

LOOKING AFTER THE VITAMINS

When father starts yawning at six in the evening, when mother has to struggle to keep awake at the kitchen sink after lunch, then it is pretty plain that the great spring malaise has arrived.

These symptoms of general fatigue which usually appear at the end of February need not be accepted as unavoidable for they are largely the result of a prolonged shortage of vitamins, especially of vitamin C. Preventive action should begin at the height of winter and the family diet be planned in such a way as to contain sufficient vitamins. 'The fight against spring fatigue begins in the kitchen in early January' is how one well-known doctor put it. So it is up to us housewives, as the family's 'vitamin managers', to see to it that our loved ones do not arrive at winter's end in a state of weariness and exhaustion, but remain as fit and as energetic as at any other time of the year.

In earlier centuries sailors used to succumb to the dreaded scurvy when subjected to long sea voyages without fresh vegetables. We suffer from a milder form of deficiency disease if our vitamin intake in winter falls below minimum require-

VITAMINS IN FRUIT

Fresh fruit	Vitamins per 100 (g.)				Intake necessary to provide daily requirement of vitamin C (g.)
	A (mg.)	B (mg.)	C (mg.)	D (J)	
Almond		0·16			
Apple		0·08	15		1,000
Apricot			12		
Banana		0·10	8		
Bilberry	1·6		10		
Blackberry	0·8		22		
Blackcurrant			100		
Cherry (black)	0·6		15		500
Cherry (red)			5		
Cranberry			15		
Grape		trace	5		2,500
Hazelnut		0·40			
Lemon			100		150–200
Orange		0·08	100		150–200
Peach			8		500
Pear		0.06	3		2,500
Plum		0·08	.		1,000
Prune		0·18	8		
Quince			15		
Raspberry			25		250
Redcurrant			16		160–200
Rosehip			500		15–20
Strawberry			50		100–200
Walnut		0·30			

16

ments; but such suffering is quite unnecessary if we make use of the supplies of citrus fruits and green vegetables in the shops all year round. A glass of orange juice, a grapefruit or a plateful of muesli in the morning, will supply most of the vitamin C our bodies need. Even stored apples contain vitamin C, although this diminishes rapidly at the beginning of spring. Blackcurrant juice and sea buckthorn syrup (see notes) are a particularly rich source of vitamin C and should never be missing from the store cupboard.

Not only do our bodies need large quantities of vitamin C, but also a frequent and regular intake, since water-soluble vitamins cannot be stored in the body. In the preparation of fruit and vegetable dishes, great care should be taken to prevent the loss of vitamin C, which is both soluble in water and sensitive to heat. Excessive amounts of water in cooking and the reheating or keeping hot of dishes should be avoided.

For good general health, however, we need meat as well as fruit and vegetables in our daily food intake, and a mixed diet, as varied as possible, is the one to be preferred.

COMPONENT NUTRIENTS OF FRUIT

Fruit	Preparation	Protein %	Fat %	Carbohydrates %	Calories per 100 g.	Water %	Minerals %	A	B	C	D
				For energy					For defence	Vitamin	
Soft fruit											
Bilberry	fresh	0·8	—	12·1	56	83·6	0·4	5	1	2	+
Bilberry (with sugar)	cooked		—			84·9	0·5	4	1	2	+
Blackberry	fresh	1·1	—	8·6	43	84·9	0·5	5	4	4	0
Blackcurrant	fresh	1·0	—	13·3	59	79·0	0·9	3	2	5	+
Cranberry	fresh	0·7	—	11·6	57	83·7	0·3	3	3	2	+
Elderberry	fresh	2·5	—	7·1	45	80·4	0·6	4	4	4	0
Elderberry	juice		—					2	2	2	0
Gooseberry	fresh	0·9	—	8·8	46	85·5	0·5	4	1	4	0
Gooseberry (with sugar)	cooked	0·8	—	66·3	275	29·9	0·5	4	1	4	0
Grape	fresh	0·7	—	16·7	77	79·1	0·5	1	2	1	0
Raspberry	fresh	1·4	—	6·8	40	84·0	0·6	5	2	3	+
Raspberry (with sugar)	cooked	1·1	—	68·5	284	26·5	0·4	5	2	3	+
Raspberry	juice	0·4	—	8·0	37	89·6	0·5	0	2	+	+
Redcurrant	fresh	1·3	—	7·5	36	83·8	0·7	4	2	3	+

| | | For energy | | | | | | For defence | | | |
Fruit	Prepara-tion	Protein %	Fat %	Carbo-hydrates %	Calories per 100 g.	Water %	Minerals %	A	Vitamin B	C	D
Redcurrant											
(with sugar)	cooked	0·5	—	65·3	270	30·1	0·5	4	2	3	+
Redcurrant	juice	0·3	—	8·7	42	88·4	0·5	0	0	0	0
Strawberry	fresh	1·3	—	7·8	44	85·4	0·7	1	1	4	0
Strawberry											
(with sugar)	cooked	0·6	—	68·2	279	29·3	0·4	1	1	4	0
Whitecurrant	fresh	1·6	—	6·1	32	82·4	0·6	+	2	3	+
Whitecurrant											
(with sugar)	cooked	0·5	—	65·3	270	30·1	0·5	+	2	3	+
Stone fruit											
Apricot	fresh	0·9	—	11·1	54	85·2	0·7	2	2	1	0
Cherry, white	fresh	1 2	—	8 6	40	82·5	0·8	2	1	2	+
Cherry, red, early	fresh	0·9	—	10·3	46	81·2	0·6	2	1	2	÷
Cherry,											
black, large	fresh	1·0	—	10·7	48	79·7	0·6	4	3	3	+
Cherry, morello	fresh	0·8	—	8·8	39	80·5	0·6	4	2	3	+
Cherry											
(with sugar)	cooked	1·0	—	68·4	281	28·7	0·7	3	2	2	+
Cherry	juice	0·5	—	16·0	69	82·4	0·5	2	1	1	+
Peach	fresh	0·8	—	14·2	64	82·7	0·6	2	2	1	0
Plum, blue, large	fresh	0·8	—	16·8	75	80·4	0·5	3	2	1	0
Plum (with sugar)	cooked	0·8	—	66·6	274	30·2	0·4	3	2	1	0
Plum, red, small	fresh	0·6	—	12·1	52	83·4	0·5	1	2	1	0
Plum, Mirabelle	fresh	0·8	—	16·4	73	80·7	0·5	3	2	2	0
Plum, Reine Claude	fresh	0·8	—	15·9	72	81·9	0·6	4	2	4	0
Plum, switzen	fresh	0·7	—	15·7	69	81·8	0·5	4	2	1	0
Plum (compote)	cooked	1·5	—	54·8	232	39·6	0·9	4	2	1	0
Other fruit											
Apple, average	fresh	0·4	—	13·3	58	83·9	0·4	2	1	2	0
Apple, cooking	fresh							2	1	2	0
Apple, dessert								2	1	3	0
Apple (compote)	cooked	0·4	—	23·2	97	75·9	0·4	2	+	1	0
Apple	juice	0·3	—	15·0	67	83·8	0·5	2	1	+	0
Lemon	fresh	0·7	—	8·4	50	82·6	0·6	3	2	5	0
Lemon	juice	0·3	—	2·7	29	89·7	0·5	3	2	5	0
Orange	fresh	0·8	—	12·6	58	84·3	0·5	4	2	5	0
Pear, average	fresh	0·4	—	13·6	58	82·8	0·4	1	1	1	0
Quince	fresh	0·6	—	14·2	60	81·9	0·6			2	0
Rosehip	dried	4·1	0·7	62·2	310	12·5	3·3	3	2	5	0
Nuts											
Almond	fresh	21·4	53·2	13·2	646	6·3	2·3	1	4		
Chestnut	fresh	6·1	4·1	39·7	225	47·0	1·4	1	2		
Hazlenut	fresh	17·4	62·6	7·2	691	7·1	2·5	1	4		
Walnut, green	fresh									5	
Walnut, ripe	fresh	16·7	58·5	13·0	673	7·2	1·7	1	5		

These tables are reprinted by kind permission of the publishers Bechtold & Co., Wiesbaden and Eugen Ulmer, Stuttgart, from the series 'Kurzrezepte für den Gartenbau' Nr. 4 (out of print).

ETIQUETTE OF SERVING AND EATING FRUIT

Nature showers us with its bounty of the most varied kinds of fruit – home-grown and imported – all the year round and many meals, from the formal banquet to the simple family meal, are rounded off with fresh fruit. Guests are sometimes embarrassed because they do not know how various fruits should be eaten. So here are a few hints to help the hostess.

Soft fruits should be served in individual fruit bowls and eaten with a small spoon. Large gooseberries (unsugared) can be picked up and eaten with the fingers.

With peaches every guest should be handed a fruit knife and fork. To eat, cut the fruit in half, remove the stone with the fork, then continue to eat with knife and fork. Do not touch the fruit with your fingers.

Apricots, plums and switzen plums should be squeezed open by pressing them gently at both ends over a plate. Remove the stone with a small spoon and eat the flesh with your fingers.

Fruit knives will again be necessary when serving apples or pears. The fruit should be arranged in a bowl or fruit basket. Take one with your hand, transfer it to your plate, halve and core the fruit with the knife and eat it, peeled or unpeeled, with your fingers.

Grapes should be washed and separated into convenient sprigs with kitchen scissors before serving. Hold the sprig in your left hand, pick off the grapes with the fingers of your right, and eat.

Oranges are served in the same way as apples and pears. Peel the fruit with a fruit knife either in the customary way or – more artistically – by making incisions with the point of the knife round the orange in such a way that the skin can be peeled back to resemble the petals of a water lily. Remove the pith. The quarters will come away easily and are eaten with the fingers.

Fresh pineapples and melons should be halved and in melons the seeds should be removed with a spoon. The fruit is then served cut into thick slices on individual plates. Guests cut the flesh with fruit knives and forks and eat it with silver or stainless steel spoons. Tinned pineapples are served in fruit dishes and eaten with dessert spoons.

Bananas are easy to serve and to eat. Break or cut off the tip of the skin with a knife and then 'unzip' the skin to near the base where a natural 'handle' should be preserved.

Compote should be served in fruit bowls standing on a plate and eaten with a small spoon. Stones should be put on to the plate, also the spoon.

Notes to the English Edition

Ingredients

All the ingredients used in the recipes in this book are available in this country now that more and more delicatessen shops are being opened in cities and towns. In addition, the food departments of large stores are often able to supply some of the more unusual items; some London shops run a postal service. For those in shopping difficulties, however, there are very good substitutes available in most good grocery shops which should produce excellent results.

Gelatine. The German Food Centre in Knightsbridge, and Schmidts in Charlotte Street, W.1. (who supply by post), stock leaf gelatine; it is also worth enquiring at the food department of your local store. Failing that, you will obtain equally good results with powdered gelatine. As there are slight variations in the stiffening properties of individual brands it is best to follow the makers' instructions for the amount of liquid given in the recipe (5 leaves gelatine = 5 teaspoons powdered gelatine = $\frac{1}{2}$ ounce).

Potato flour. This is the usual thickening agent used by continental cooks in soups, gravies, etc., and it can be bought under a French trade name in stores and delicatessen shops. British housewives will be more familiar with cornflour, which it closely resembles; this can be used in all recipes stipulating potato flour as an ingredient.

Sea buckthorn syrup. This vitamin-rich syrup, which is freely available in German shops, is also stocked in many of the health-food stores in Britain. It is similar to rose-hip syrup both in flavour and vitamin content and the latter can be used as a substitute for it.

Vanilla sugar. The small packets of Dr Oetker vanilla sugar available in continental grocery stores, can be obtained in many of the more specialized shops in this country. Alternatively, vanilla sugar can be easily made by keeping a vanilla pod broken up into pieces in a screw-top jar containing 2 lb. of icing or castor sugar. The same pod can be used for 2 months.

Temperature Chart

	Degrees F	*Regulo gas*
Very slow	240–280	$\frac{1}{4}$–$\frac{1}{2}$
Slow	280–320	1
Warm	320–340	3
Moderate	340–370	4
Fairly hot	370–400	5–6
Hot	400–440	7
Very hot	440–480	8–9

Units of Measurement

	British		*Metric*
	pkt.	packet(s)	
oz.	ounce(s)	mg.	milligramme(s)
lb.	pound(s)	g.	gramme(s)
		kg.	kilogramme(s)

$$1 \text{ oz.} \approx 30 \text{ g.}$$
$$1 \text{ lb.} \approx 450 \text{ g.}$$

	British		*Metric*
fl. oz.	fluid ounces(s)	l.	litre(s)
pt.	pint(s)		

$$35 \text{ fl. oz.} = 1\tfrac{3}{4} \text{ pt.} \approx 1 \text{ litre}$$

| tsp. | teaspoon(s) |
| tbsp. | tablespoon(s) |

All spoon measures given in the recipes are British and refer to level spoonfuls, unless otherwise indicated. Their metric equivalents may be calculated from:

$2\frac{1}{2}$ British tsp./tbsp. $\approx$ 3 metric tsp./tbsp.

Note: 3 tsp. = 1 tbsp. (British and metric)

Within each recipe, both British and metric measures are given. Although the measures are not always exactly equal, the proportions of the ingredients remain the same in both cases.

N.B. All recipes are for 4 people unless otherwise stated.

Start the Day with Fruit

For general wellbeing and a slim figure we should start the day with a glass of fruit juice and a plateful of muesli for breakfast. Swiss Bircher-Benner muesli has already won a firm place for itself on countless breakfast tables. It is based on a health-giving mixture of oats, fruit and nuts to which rye bread, wholemeal bread or one of the proprietary pumpernickel breads available in many delicatessen stores forms the ideal accompaniment. All fruit consumed raw should be washed first.

For the following recipes most kinds of fruit in season are suitable and, of course, deep frozen ones can be used all the year round. A food mixer with blender attachment is useful, but in many recipes nothing more elaborate than a fork is required and some hand-operated presses are on the market for extracting fruit juices.

Mueslis should not be kept waiting but eaten at once; they discolour easily and so do not look attractive.

One further tip: where milk shakes are flavoured with lemon or orange, this should be added slowly, drop by drop, to prevent curdling.

Quantities in this chapter are for one person.

Morning Cup
(MOGENTRUNK)

Ingredients: Unsweetened stewed rhubarb, sugar, lemon juice.

Rub the rhubarb through a sieve, sweeten the resulting juice to taste. Add ¾ teaspoon lemon juice to each glass of juice.

This juice taken first thing in the morning stimulates the digestive system.

Rhubarb Milk
(RHABARBERMILCH)

Ingredients: 1 glass milk, 3 tbsp. rhubarb juice.

Mix the well chilled juice gradually with the milk.

Lemon or Orange Milk
(ZITRONEN- ODER ORANGENMILCH)

Ingredients: 1 glass milk (scalded and chilled), juice of ½–1 lemon or orange, 1¾ tsp. sugar.

Mix the juice and sugar with the milk and serve well chilled in summer, at room temperature in winter.

Banana Milk
(BANANENMILCH)

Ingredients: ¼–½ banana, 1¾ tsp. grated hazelnuts, 1 glass milk.

Mash the banana with a fork and mix with milk or put into electric blender. Serve with nuts (or a little grated chocolate) sprinkled on top. In hot weather add an ice cube.

Carrot and Orange Cup
(KAROTTEN-ORANGENSAFT)

Ingredients: Juice of 2 oranges, 4 carrots, juice of ½ lemon, ¾ tsp. sugar or honey.

Clean the carrots, cut them into strips and put them through a juice extractor, or place into blender together with the peeled oranges. Add remaining ingredients to the combined juices and serve chilled.

Strawberry Yogurt
(ERDBEER-JOGHURTBECHER)

Ingredients: ¼ pt. (⅛ l.) yogurt, 5–6 oz. (150 g.) strawberries, sugar, 1 pkt. (1½ tbsp.) vanilla sugar, few drops rum or rum essence.

Cut the strawberries into small pieces, mix with the yogurt, add sugars to taste and flavour with rum.

Yogurt with Redcurrants or Blackcurrants
(JOGHURTBECHER MIT ROTEN ODER SCHWARZEN JOHANNISBEEREN)

Ingredients: ¼ pt. (⅛ l.) yogurt, 2½ tsp. sea buckthorn syrup, 3½ oz. (100 g.) redcurrants or blackcurrants, 2½ tsp. desiccated coconut.

Mix the syrup with the yogurt and add the washed and prepared currants. Pour the mixture into a tall glass, sprinkle with coconut and serve with wholemeal bread.

Yogurt with Peaches
(JOGHURT MIT PFIRSCHEN)

Ingredients: ¼ pt. (⅛ l.) yogurt, 1 peach, juice of ½ lemon, 2–3 tbsp. sugar, grated chocolate.

Stone the peach and mash with a fork or put through a mixer. Mix with yogurt and add lemon juice and sugar. Sprinkle chocolate on top to delight children of all ages.

Fruit Yogurt
(JOGHURTMIXEREI)

Ingredients: ¼ pt. (⅛ l.) yogurt, 4–5 oz. (100–150 g.) fresh berries or ½ banana or 1 orange, sugar.

Clean and chop the fruit, whip the yogurt, add the fruit and sugar to taste.

Stewed rhubarb can be substituted for the berries.

Yogurt with Banana
(BANANEN-JOGHURT)

Ingredients: ¼ pt. (⅛ l.) yogurt, ¼–½ banana, ¾ tsp. orange juice.

Pulp banana with fork or in mixer, mix with whipped yogurt and flavour with orange juice.

Yogurt with Cranberries
(JOGHURT MIT PREISELBEEREN)

Ingredients: ¼ pt. (⅛ l.) yogurt, 3 tbsp. cranberry compote, grated orange rind.

Whip the yogurt, add the cranberries or put through the blender first for extra smoothness, flavour with orange rind. Blend in a peach or 1–2 tablespoons stewed apples for additional flavour.

MUESLIS

Bircher-Benner Muesli
(Original recipe)
(BIRCHER-BENNER-MÜSLI)

Ingredients: 2½ tsp. oatmeal, 2½ tbsp. water, 2½ tsp. lemon juice, 2½ tsp. condensed milk, 7 oz. (200 g.) apples, 1½–2 tbsp. chopped nuts or almonds.

Mix the oatmeal with the water, milk and lemon juice, wash and grate the apples and add to the mixture. Sprinkle the nuts on top and serve immediately.

Oatmeal Muesli
(HAFERFLOCKENMÜSLI)

Ingredients: 1½–2 tbsp. oatmeal, ¼ pt. (⅛ l.) milk, 3½ oz. (100 g.) fresh or frozen fruit (berries, currants, peaches, apricots, greengages, apples, oranges, bananas, etc.), sugar and honey, 1½–2 tbsp. chopped hazelnuts.

Put oatmeal into a dish, pour on the milk, cut fruit to a convenient size and arrange on top, sweeten if necessary and serve sprinkled with chopped nuts.

Yogurt can be substituted for the milk and crumbled biscuit for the oatmeal. A refreshing summer dish.

Apple Muesli
(APFELMÜSLI)

Ingredients: 2 apples, 1 tbsp. sugar, juice of 1 lemon, 1½–2 tbsp. chopped almonds or hazelnuts.

Grate the peeled or unpeeled apples, sprinkle with lemon juice immediately to prevent discoloration. Sweeten to taste, sprinkle nuts or almonds on top and serve immediately.

Apple and Orange Muesli
(APFEL-ORANGEN-MÜSLI)

Ingredients: 1 apple, 1 orange, juice of ½ lemon, 2–3 tsp. sugar.

Grate the apple and sprinkle with lemon juice. Peel the orange, remove pith and chop up very small. Mix with the apple and sweeten to taste.

Carrot Muesli
(KAROTTEN-MÜSLI)

Ingredients: 9 oz. (250 g.) carrots, 1 apple, pinch of sugar, 2½ tbsp. yogurt.

Clean and grate carrots and the peeled or unpeeled apple. Stir in yogurt and sweeten.

Beetroot Muesli
(ROTE-BEETE-MÜSLI)

Ingredients: 1 small raw beetroot, 1 medium apple, pinch of sugar, juice of ½ lemon, 4 fl. oz. ($\frac{1}{10}$ l.) sour cream, 1½–2 tbsp. oatmeal.

Peel and grate the beetroot and the apple, mix, add sugar and lemon juice to taste. Pour cream over and sprinkle with the oatmeal. Serve immediately.

Beetroot is rich in vitamins A, B and C.

Banana Muesli
(BANANEN-MÜSLI)

Ingredients: 1 banana, juice of ½ lemon, 2–3 tsp. sugar, 1½–2 tbsp. oatmeal fried in butter.

Mash the banana with a fork, sprinkle with lemon juice, then with sugar and oatmeal.

Instead of sugar, this muesli can be sweetened with honey, and enriched in vitamin A content by the addition of a grated carrot.

Served with pumpernickel, this dish is especially recommended for children.

BREAKFAST DISHES WITH FRESH FRUIT

Breakfast Porridge with Fruit
(FRÜHSTÜCKSBREI MIT OBSTMARK)

Ingredients: Scant ½ pt. (¼ l.) milk, 5½ oz. (150 g.) flour, 1 banana or 3½ oz. (100 g.) pulped berries or currants.

Put flour into a saucepan, add a little of the milk and stir until smooth, add the remainder of the milk, bring to the boil and simmer for 3 minutes, stirring constantly. Take off the heat and blend with the prepared fruit.

Cornflakes with Fruit
(CORNFLAKES MIT OBST)

Ingredients: 3–5 tbsp. cornflakes, 5–7 oz. (150–200 g.) redcurrants or other soft fruit or 1 banana, sugar.

Pulp the fruit, rub gooseberries or currants through a sieve. Arrange fruit on a dish, add sugar and cornflakes.

Health Dish with Oatmeal
(FLOCKENGESUNDHEITSSPEISE)

Ingredients: 3 tbsp. oatmeal, 3 tbsp. coconut, 3 tbsp. sultanas or raisins, 3 tbsp. sugar, little grated lemon rind.

Wash the sultanas or raisins and leave to soak for a few hours. Mix all the ingredients together.

This breakfast dish may also be served with stewed fruit, fruit salad or a grated apple.

Breakfast Fruit Salad
(FRÜHSTÜCKS-OBSTSALAT)

Ingredients: ½ orange, ½ apple, 1 tbsp. sultanas, 2 figs, 1½–2 tbsp. grated nuts, juice of 1 lemon.

Prepare the fruit, cut into small pieces and mix.

Condensed milk may be used instead of sugar to sweeten the salad, and it can be served in orange or grapefruit 'baskets' by halving the fruit, scooping out the flesh and piling the salad in the shells.

Health Dish with Apples
(APFEL-ROHKOST)

Ingredients: 4–5 large apples (preferably Bramleys), sugar, juice of 1 lemon and 1 orange, ½ pt. (¼ l.) condensed milk.

Peel and grate the apples and mix with the fruit juices. Sweeten, stir in the milk and serve at once.

This dish is also suitable for a snack between meals, as an accompaniment to roast pork or chicken, or as part of a special diet. It can be served and sprinkled with 1 tablespoon of oatmeal fried in butter.

Strawberry Cup
(ERDBEER-ROHKOST)

Ingredients: 5–7 oz. (150–200 g.) strawberries, sugar, ¼ pt. (⅛ l.) yogurt, 2 slices grated pumpernickel or dark rye bread.

Wash the strawberries and rub them through a sieve. Stir the fruit pulp into the yogurt and serve sprinkled with grated bread.

Banana Breakfast
(BANANEN-TELLERSPEISE)

Ingredients: 1–2 bananas, 2½–5 tsp. sea buckthorn syrup, lemon juice, 1½ tbsp. grated chocolate.

Mash the bananas with a fork, add sea buckthorn syrup and lemon juice to taste. Sprinkle chocolate on top and serve.

Curd Cheese with Fruit
(QUARK MIT OBST)

Ingredients: 3½–5 oz. (100–150 g.) curd cheese, 1½ tbsp. milk, 1 banana, juice of ½ lemon, 1 pkt. (1½ tbsp.) vanilla sugar.

Cream the curd cheese with the milk, add the pulped banana and sugar and lemon juice to taste.

For the bananas, cherries (7 ounces [200 grammes] stoned), strawberries or raspberries, an orange or grated apple may be substituted. Honey can be used for sweetening, and the stiffly beaten white of an egg, folded in just before serving improves the dish.

Curd Cheese with Banana
(BANANENQUARK)

Ingredients: 5 oz. (150 g.) curd cheese, 1 banana, ¾ tsp. lemon or orange juice, sugar.

Cream the curd cheese with the milk, add the pulped banana, beat well and flavour with sugar and fruit juice.

A grated carrot or a grated apple may be added.

Curd Cheese with Almonds and Strawberries
(MANDELQUARK MIT ERDBEEREN)

Ingredients: 9 oz. (250 g.) curd cheese, 2–3 tbsp. sugar, lemon juice, 1 oz. (25 g.) blanched and chopped almonds, 7 oz. (200 g.) strawberries.

Cream the cheese, add sugar, lemon juice and almonds. Wash the strawberries, halve and add to the mixture. Serve with bread and butter or toast.

For special occasions cut some large strawberries in half, scoop out part of the flesh with a small spoon, pile some of the almond cheese into the fruit and put the halves together again. This looks very attractive.

Curd Cheese with Apple
(APFELQUARK)

Ingredients: 5 oz. (150 g.) cream cheese, 1–2 grated apples, 2½ tsp. sea buckthorn syrup.

Cream the cheese, add the apples and stir in the sea buckthorn syrup.

The latter may be omitted and the dish flavoured with sugar, vanilla sugar or honey instead.

Gervais with Fruit
(GERVAIS MIT OBST)

Ingredients: 2 small individual packets of Gervais, 1 oz. (30 g.) butter, 1½–2 tbsp. sultanas, 1 chopped-up peach or a few grapes, sugar.

Cream the butter and cheese, add the fruit and sweeten to taste. Serve with bread or toast.

Scrambled Eggs with Fruit
(OBSTRÜHREI AUF GEWÜRZKUCHEN)

Ingredients: 2–3 apricots, 4 eggs, 1½–2 tbsp. sugar, 5 tsp. brandy, 2½ tbsp. tinned milk, pinch of salt, fat, 4 slices spiced cake.

Wash and stone the apricots, place into a dish, sprinkle with sugar and half the brandy. Leave the fruit until it has softened, then cut into thin strips. Break the eggs into a bowl, add the milk and remaining brandy and beat the mixture well. Heat fat in a pan, pour in the egg mixture and stir. When the mixture has set, add the apricot strips. Arrange the eggs on the cake.

Pears can be used instead of apricots, in which case a mixture of brandy and lemon juice should be sprinkled on the fruit to keep it white.

This is particularly suitable as a Sunday morning breakfast dish. Children love it and do not mind if more sugar is used instead of brandy.

SPREADS

Lemon Butter
(ZITRONENBUTTER)

Ingredients: 2 oz. (60 g.) butter, juice of ½ lemon, bananas, strawberries.

Cream the butter and add the lemon juice. Spread a few slices of white and brown bread with the butter and decorate with slices of strawberries and bananas.

Alternatively, the butter can be used as a garnish for cold meats, steaks or escalopes. In this case, add some finely chopped fresh herbs, chill and shape into little balls.

Toast Sevilla
(TOASTBROT SEVILLA)

Ingredients per person: 2 slices of toast, little butter, 1 orange or 1 banana, 1½ tsp. sugar.

Butter the toast, garnish with slices of banana or orange and sprinkle with sugar.

Strawberries or raspberries may be used as an alternative, and honey substituted for the sugar.

Gourmet Butter
(SCHLEMMERBUTTER)

Ingredients: 1¾ oz. (50 g.) butter, ½ pear, 2½ tsp. grated hazelnuts, lemon juice, sugar.

Cream the butter, add the grated fruit and nuts and flavour with sugar and lemon juice to taste.

A sandwich spread which is very popular with children.

The First Course

FRUIT SOUPS

Nothing is more refreshing as a first course to a meal in summer than a chilled fruit soup. It is quick and easy to prepare and any fruit in season is suitable. A stiffly beaten egg white or small semolina dumplings can be used as garnish, or it can be served sprinkled with crumbled biscuits.

Hamburg Rhubarb Soup with Dumplings
(HAMBURGER RHABARBER-KALTSCHALE MIT SCHWAMMKLÖSSCHEN)

> *Ingredients:* 1 lb. (500 g.) rhubarb, rind of $\frac{1}{2}$ lemon, $1\frac{1}{2}$ tbsp. potato flour, 1 glass apple juice, 6–7 oz. (170–200 g.) sugar.
>
> *For the dumplings:* $\frac{1}{4}$ pt. ($\frac{1}{8}$ l.) milk, 1 oz. (30 g.) margarine, 4 oz. (120 g.) flour, 1 egg, sugar.

Clean the rhubarb, cut into pieces, put into a saucepan with the lemon rind and a little water and stew for a few minutes. Remove the lemon rind. Mix the flour to a smooth paste with a few teaspoons of water, add this to the rhubarb and simmer a little longer, stirring continuously until the mixture thickens. Finally add apple juice and sugar to taste.

For the dumplings, place the milk and margarine in a pan over a gentle heat. When the milk has boiled up once, draw aside and immediately tip in the flour. Beat until the mixture leaves the sides of the pan. Whisk the egg and beat into the mixture until smooth. Add sugar to taste. Drop teaspoonfuls of the mixture into fast boiling salted water and boil for a minute or two.

Cherry Soup
(KIRSCHSUPPE)

Ingredients: 1 lb. (500 g.) stoned cherries, 1 piece of lemon rind, ½ stick cinnamon, 1¼ oz. (40 g.) sugar, ¾ pt. (½ l.) red wine, 1 tbsp. potato flour, little grated lemon rind mixed with sugar.

Place the cherries, lemon rind, cinnamon and sugar into a saucepan, add 1¾ pints (1 litre) water and bring to the boil Simmer for about 10 minutes, then add the wine and thicken with the potato flour mixed to a smooth paste. Remove cinnamon and rind and leave to cool. Before serving sprinkle with grated rind and sugar.

Dortmund Cherry Soup
(DORTMUNDER KIRSCHSUPPE)

Ingredients: 1¼ lb. (500 g.) stoned cherries, ¼ pt. (⅛ l.) yogurt, ½ pt. (¼ l.) sour cream, 1 pt. (½ l.) milk, grated brown bread, sugar mixed with cinnamon.

Whip the yogurt, cream and milk together and add the cherries. Serve with a mixture of bread, sugar and cinnamon sprinkled on top.

Other fruits, such as raspberries, strawberries, blackberries are suitable for this soup.

Cherry Milk Soup
(KIRSCH-MILCHSUPPE)

Ingredients: 3 oz. (100 g.) grated hazelnuts, 3 oz. (100 g.) sugar, 1½ oz. (50 g.) oatmeal, 1 lb. (500 g.) stoned cherries, milk.

Gently warm as much milk as is needed and add all the other ingredients.

Soup Regina
(REGINA KALTSCHALE)

Ingredients: 1 lb. (500 g.) redcurrants, rind of ½ lemon, 2 oz. (60 g.) sugar, 1 tbsp. potato flour, 8 fl. oz. (¼ l.) white wine, crumbled biscuits for garnish.

Wash the berries, discard the stems and place into a pan, keeping a handful for garnish. Add the sugar, lemon rind and 1¼ pints (¾ litre) water. Boil for 5 minutes, then sieve. Mix the potato flour to a smooth paste with a little water, add to the fruit juice, return the mixture to the stove and boil up once more, stirring continuously. Remove from the heat and leave to cool. Add the wine just before serving and garnish with currants and crumbled biscuits.

Simple Milk Soup with Fruit
(EINFACHE MILCHSUPPE MIT OBST)

Ingredients: 2 pt. (1 l.) milk, 2 pkt. (4 tbsp.) custard powder, 14 oz. (375 g.) soft fruit, 1–2 egg whites, 7 tbsp. sugar.

Make a custard in the usual way from the milk and custard powder. Sweeten. Beat the whites until stiff and drop teaspoonfuls into the hot custard. Leave for a few moments until set, then remove with a spoon. Now add the prepared fruit to the custard, cool and garnish with the 'snowflakes'. Serve with biscuits.

Fruit in Wine Sauce
(FRÜCHTE IN WEINSAUCE)

Ingredients: 1 lb. (500 g.) mixed fruit (strawberries, raspberries, cherries, bananas), juice of 2 lemons, 1 oz. (30 g.) blanched and chopped almonds, sugar or vanilla sugar.

For the wine sauce: 2 eggs, 1 pt. (½ l.) white wine or apple juice, 2–3 tbsp. sugar.

Wash and trim the fruit and, if using cherries and bananas, stone the former and slice the latter. Arrange in a glass bowl, sprinkle first with lemon juice, then with sugar and almonds.

For the sauce, put the ingredients into a saucepan, beat with a whisk and place over another pan of boiling water. Beat continuously until frothy and firm. Pour over the fruit or serve separately.

Strawberries in Wine
(WEINKALTSCHALE MIT ERDBEEREN)

Ingredients: 1½ pt. (1 l.) white wine, 1 lb. (500 g.) strawberries, sugar.

Pour the wine into a deep bowl, wash and chop the strawberries and add, sweeten to taste and chill. Delicious on a hot day.

Coconut with Fruit
(FLOCKEN-KALTSCHALE)

Ingredients: About 1½ lb. (500–750 g.) strawberries or other soft fruit, 4–5 oz. (100–150 g.) sugar, 2–3 oz. (60–80 g.) desiccated coconut, 2¼ pt. (1¼ l.) milk.

Wash and halve the strawberries, add the sugar and leave until juice has formed. Add the coconut, mix well and pour chilled milk over the dish.

Cold Gooseberry Soup
(KALTESTACHELBEERSUPPE)

Ingredients: Gooseberry compote made from 1¼ lb. (500 g.) fruit, sugar, 3 pt. (1½ l.) milk, 3 pkt. (6 tbsp.) custard power, 2 grated sponge fingers.

Prepare the custard, cool and serve with the chilled fruit. Sprinkle with sponge fingers.

Worms Strawberry Soup
(WORMSER ERDBEER-KALTSCHALE)

Ingredients: 2½ pt. (1½ l.) milk, 1¾ lb. (750 g.) strawberries, sugar, 1 pkt. (1½ tbsp.) vanilla sugar.

Wash the strawberries, halve the large ones and put into a deep
bowl. Sugar well. Flavour the milk with vanilla sugar to taste
and pour over the fruit. Serve chilled.

Students' Soup
(STUDENTEN-KALTSCHALE)

Ingredients: 2¼ lb. (1 kg.) soft fruit (strawberries, redcurrants,
     gooseberries, raspberries, bilberries or black-
     berries), 2½ pt. (1½ l.) sour milk, sugar, cinnamon.

Wash and prepare the fruit and put into soup cups. Pour on
the milk and sprinkle with sugar and cinnamon.

 This refreshing dish can be served as a first course or to con-
clude a summer meal.

Fruit Soup Duet
(OBSTSUPPE-DUETT)

Ingredients: 10½ oz. (300 g.) redcurrants, 10½ oz. (300 g.) goose-
     berries, 8 fl. oz. (¼ l.) white wine, lemon rind,
     7 tbsp. sugar, 2–3 tsp. potato flour.

Wash and prepare the fruit, put into a pan with the sugar, rind,
wine and 1¾ pints (1 litre) water, and boil for a few minutes.
Remove from the heat and rub through a sieve. Mix the potato
flour to a smooth paste with a little water, thicken the soup and
add a little more sugar and lemon juice if necessary. Can be
served hot or chilled.

Fruit Juice Soup with Banana
(FRUCHTSAFTSUPPE MIT BANANEN)

Ingredients: 1½–2 pt. (¾–1 l.) currant juice, sugar, 2–4 tsp.
     potato flour, 2 bananas, slices of lemon.

Sweeten the currant juice to taste, slowly bring to the boil and
thicken with the potato flour. Add the sliced banana and 1 slice
of lemon per person. Serve hot or cold.

Zürich Rice Soup
(ZÜRICHER REISSUPPE)

Ingredients: 2¾ oz. (80 g.) pudding rice, 5–7 oz. (150–200 g.)
     sugar, 1 stick cinnamon, 1 lb. (500 g.) goose-
     berries, rind of ½ lemon.

Wash the rice and cook it with a little sugar and half the cinnamon stick in water until tender but not too soft. Clean and cook the gooseberries in a separate pan in a little water with sugar and the remaining cinnamon and the lemon rind. Before serving put the rice into individual dishes and pour the sieved gooseberry juice over. Alternatively, the gooseberry compote may be left whole and spooned on top of the rice, but do not forget to remove the cinnamon and lemon rind first.

Gooseberry Soup
(STACHELBEERKALTSCHALE)

Ingredients: 1¼ pt. (¾ l.) buttermilk, 1½ oz. (40 g.) potato flour, 9 oz. (250 g.) gooseberries, sugar.

Stir the potato flour into half the buttermilk and bring to the boil, stirring all the time. Wash and trim the fruit and add, together with the remainder of the milk. Boil up once more, remove from the stove and leave to cool. Serve chilled with biscuits.

Red Buttermilk Soup
(ROTE BUTTERMILCH-KALTSCHALE)

Ingredients: 9 oz. (250 g.) each of strawberries and raspberries, 1¾ pt. (1 l.) buttermilk, milk, a little butter, 2½ oz. (75 g.) oatmeal, 1 oz. (20–30 g.) sugar.

Put the cleaned fruit into a bowl or individual dishes and mix with sugar. Stir a little sweet milk into the buttermilk and pour over the fruit. Melt the butter in a pan, stir in the oatmeal with a little sugar and fry until crisp. Sprinkle over the fruit and serve.

Other fruit in season may be used for this soup.

Red and White Soup
(KALTSCHALE ROT-WEISS)

Ingredients: 2¼ pt. (1¼ l.) milk, 2 pkt. (4 tbsp.) custard powder, 8 tbsp. sugar, vanilla essence, 1¼ lb. (500–625 g.) raspberries, 1 pkt. (1½ tbsp.) vanilla sugar.

Make the custard in the usual way, adding the sugar and the vanilla essence. Leave to cool. Clean the raspberries, sweeten with vanilla sugar and ordinary sugar if desired. Pour the chilled custard over the fruit and serve.

Blue and White Soup
(KALTSCHALE BLAU-WEISS)
The same ingredients as in the previous recipe but substitute bilberries for the raspberries.

Bilberries are also delicious served simply with sugar and cold milk.

Bilberry Soup
(BLAUBEERENSUPPE)

Ingredients: 2 pt. (1 l.) milk, 15 oz. (375 g.) bilberries, 2 pkt. (4 tbsp.) custard powder, 10 tbsp. sugar, desiccated coconut.

Make the custard, leave to cool. Wash and prepare the bilberries and add to the custard just before serving. Serve coconut on a separate dish for the guests to help themselves.

Holstein Peach Soup
(HOLSTEINER PFIRSICH-KALTSCHALE)

Ingredients: 2¼ lb. (1 kg.) peaches, rind of 1 lemon, sugar, custard made from 1 pkt. (2 tbsp.) custard powder, white wine.

Blanch peaches and lemon rind. Cut peaches into quarters, remove stones and cook with the rind in a little water until soft. Sieve, sweeten to taste and add to the made-up custard. Flavour with wine just before serving.

This recipe can be used for apricots instead of peaches.

Blackberry Soup
(BROMBEER-KALTSCHALE)

Ingredients: 1¾ lb. (750 g.) blackberries, 1–2 apples, 6 tbsp. sugar, ½ stick cinnamon, 3½–5 tsp. potato flour, 1 egg white, 2–3 tsp. icing sugar.

Clean the berries and wash and slice the apples. Put into a pan with 1¼ pints (¾ litre) water, add cinnamon and bring to the boil. Rub through a sieve, sweeten to taste and thicken with the potato flour mixed to a paste. Boil up once more, stirring continuously. Draw aside. Have ready the stiffly beaten egg white to which the icing sugar has been added. Put spoonfuls of this meringue on top of the soup. Cover the pan with a lid and leave for 10 minutes. Garnish the soup with whole blackberries and serve cold.

Plum Soup Aurelia
(ZWETSCHGENSUPPE AURELIA)

Ingredients: 1¾ lb. (500–750 g.) plums, 2 pkt. (4 tbsp.) custard powder, 2 pt. (1 l.) milk, sugar.

Make up a thin custard, wash the plums (switzen-type for preference) and cook gently in the custard, until the skins burst. The fruit should remain whole. Sweeten to taste and serve chilled.

Fruit in Buttermilk
(FRÜCHTE IN BUTTERMILCH)

Ingredients: ½ lb. (250 g.) switzen plums, ½ lb. (250 g.) cooked dried pears, 1¾ pt. (1 l.) buttermilk, sugar.

Wash, stone and halve the plums. Put all the fruit into a deep bowl or into individual dishes. Pour the buttermilk over the fruit and sweeten to taste.

Other fruits in season can be used for this soup.

Grape Soup
(TRAUBEN-KALTSCHALE)

Ingredients: 1½ lb. (500–750 g.) grapes, 2–3 tsp. potato flour, sugar, 1 banana, 1 egg white, icing sugar.

Wash the grapes, put a handful aside and place the rest into a pan with 1¼ pints (1 litre) water. Bring to the boil and simmer until the fruit is soft. Rub through a sieve and thicken the resulting juice with the flour. Sweeten to taste and bring once more to the boil. When cool, pour into serving dishes and add the remaining grapes and the sliced banana. Beat the egg white stiffly, sweeten with icing sugar and garnish the soup with teaspoonfuls of the meringue mixture.

Pear Soup
(BIRNENKALTSCHALE)

Ingredients: 2–3 lb. (1–1½ kg.) juicy pears, juice of 1 lemon, 1–1½ tsp. potato flour, white wine, sugar.

Peel and core the pears and cut into small pieces. Cook in about 2½ pints (1½ litres) water until tender. Drain. Sieve the fruit and put the fruit purée into a dish. Thicken the juice with the potato flour and bring to the boil. Take off the heat and flavour with lemon juice, wine and sugar to taste. Pour over the purée and garnish with chopped almonds or 'snowflakes' (meringue mixture).

Apple Soup
(APFELSUPPE)

Ingredients: 1 lb. (500 g.) apples, 1 piece cinnamon, 4 oz. (125 g.) sugar, 3½ tbsp. semolina, apple juice.

Peel, core and slice the apples. Put the slices into a pan with the sugar and cinnamon, add a little water and cook until tender. Drain the liquid and add apple juice (or white wine if preferred) to make up 1¾ pints (1 litre). Stir in the semolina, bring to the boil and simmer for a few moments until the soup thickens. Add the apple slices and serve hot or cold.

Rumanian Apple Soup
(RUMÄNISCHE APFELSUPPE)

Ingredients: Left-over stewed apples, sugar, a little condensed milk, grated rind of ½ lemon or orange, red wine.

Sieve the apples, sweeten and add the remaining ingredients. Serve chilled and hand round biscuits.

Apples in Buttermilk
(ÄPFEL IN BUTTERMILCH)

Ingredients: 4 cooking apples, 4 slices wholemeal bread, 1¾ pt.
(1 l.) buttermilk, salt, 3 slices pumpernickel, sugar.

Peel, core and slice the apples thinly. Add the apples to the
buttermilk together with the crumbled bread and a pinch of
salt. Bring to the boil and cook until the apples are tender.
Pour into a serving dish and sprinkle with sugar—brown or
demerara for preference—and the crumbled pumpernickel.

Budapest Fruit Soup
(BUDAPESTER OBSTSUPPE)

Ingredients: 1¾ pt. (1 l.) tomato soup, 2 apples.

Peel and dice the apples and add to the hot tomato soup.

Cold Orange Soup
(KALTE ORANGENSUPPE)

Ingredients: 1¾ pt. (1 l.) beef tea, 2 cloves, juice of 1–2 oranges,
grated rind of ½ orange.

Add the cloves to the hot beef tea and boil for a few minutes.
Remove cloves and leave soup to cool. When cold, add the
orange juice and sprinkle with grated rind. Serve in individual
cups or dishes and garnish each with a slice of orange. Tastes
very refreshing.

Breslau Pumpkin Soup
(BRESLAUER KÜRBISSUPPE)

Ingredients: 1 pumpkin, 2 rolls, ½ vanilla pod, few cloves, nutmeg, ¾–1 pt. (½ l.) milk, ¾ oz. (20 g.) potato flour,
sugar, salt, butter.

Cut the pumpkin in half, remove the flesh, dice it and put into
a pan, together with the pips chopped up small. Add ¾–1 pint
(½ litre) water, the vanilla pod, cloves and nutmeg and cook
until tender. Rub through a sieve. Break the rolls into small
pieces, moisten with water, squeeze out surplus and add to the
fruit pulp. Dilute 1¾ pints (1 litre) of it with the milk. Bring to
the boil once more, bind with potato flour and flavour with
salt and sugar. Pour melted butter over the soup.

44

Quince Soup
(QUITTENSUPPE)

Ingredients: 5 quinces, $\frac{3}{4}$–1 pt. ($\frac{1}{2}$ l.) white wine, sugar, cinnamon.

Brush the quinces, remove stems, quarter, place in a saucepan
and cover with water. Cook until tender and rub through a
sieve. Dilute with water or wine. Boil up once more, flavour
with sugar and cinnamon and serve garnished with 'snowflakes' (meringue mixture).

FRUIT AND VEGETABLE SALADS

With salads, presentation is particularly important and any
salad, fruit, vegetable or a combination of the two should pre-
sent a feast for the eyes as well as for the tastebuds. When you
start a meal with salad, an hors d'oeuvre which, we are told,
was already the ancient Greeks' choice, in preference to soup,
you stimulate your guests' appetites without burdening their
stomachs. Remember that with few exceptions, salads should
be prepared and served immediately.

Three-Fruits Salad
(DREIFRUCHT-SALAT)

Ingredients: 1 lb. (500 g.) strawberries, sugar, juice of 2
oranges, 4 pineapple rings.

Prepare, wash and halve the strawberries. Rub half the fruit
through a sieve and flavour with orange juice and sugar. Mix
with the remaining fruit and arrange on the pineapple rings.

Peach Salad
(PFIRSICH-SALAT)

Ingredients: 4–5 large yellow peaches, 5 tsp. sea buckthorn
syrup, 1 tin condensed milk or the equivalent
amount of cream, 1 pkt. ($1\frac{1}{2}$ tbsp.) vanilla sugar,
chopped nuts or almonds.

Peel, halve and slice the peaches thinly. Sprinkle with vanilla sugar. Mix with the sea buckthorn syrup and pour the cream over.

Garnish with chopped nuts or almonds if desired.

Orange Salad Valencia
(ORANGENSALAT VALENCIA)

Ingredients: 1 small lettuce, 2–3 small oranges, vinegar, salad oil, salt, 1 egg yolk, tinned milk.

Wash the lettuce, arrange on a dish and sprinkle with oil. Peel the oranges, slice thinly and arrange on the lettuce. Make a dressing from 1 part vinegar, 3 parts oil, a pinch of salt, the beaten yolk and milk. Pour over the salad.

Serve as an accompaniment with game, poultry and veal dishes.

Californian Salad
(KALIFORNISCHER SALAT)

Ingredients: 4–5 tomatoes, 1 banana, 1 pear, 4 sliced or chopped oranges or mandarins, 1 apple, 4 fl. oz. ($\frac{1}{10}$ l.) sour cream, juice of 1 lemon, salt, paprika.

Slice the tomatoes thinly, peel and dice the banana, pear and apple. Add the chopped mandarin slices and arrange on a dish. Make a dressing from the sour cream, lemon juice and seasonings and pour over the salad.

Variations of this dish are possible. For example, the salad can be piled into the scooped-out tomatoes and served on a bed of lettuce. In this case, do not add the tomato pulp to the salad.

Salad à la Johnny
(SALAT À LA JONNY)

Ingredients: $\frac{3}{4}$ lb. (375 g.) cooked asparagus, 2 hard-boiled eggs, 8–10 stoned olives, 1 apple, 5 tbsp. mayonnaise, $1\frac{1}{2}$–2 tbsp. white wine.

Cut the asparagus into small pieces, peel the apple and dice. Chop the eggs and olives very small and mix everything well together. Thin the mayonnaise with the wine, pour over the salad.

For a salad less rich in calories, omit the mayonnaise and use only the wine as a dressing.

Red Pepper Salad
(UNGARISCHER ROTER PAPRIKASALAT)

Ingredients: 10½ oz. (300 g.) sweet red peppers, 2 apples, 2–3 sticks celery or ½ celeriac, juice of 2 lemons, 3 tbsp. oil, 5 tsp. vinegar, salt, thick mayonnaise or white of 1 hard-boiled egg.

Cut a round piece off the top of each pepper, remove pips and wash the shell out well. Peel the apples and cut them, the peppers and the celery into strips. Sprinkle with lemon juice and mix. Make a salad dressing from the vinegar, oil and salt and combine with the salad. Garnish with a little thick mayonnaise or the finely chopped egg white.

Colourful Salad
(BUNTER SALAT)

Ingredients: 1 lettuce, 1 carrot, 2 pineapple rings, ½ orange, 4 fl. oz. ($\frac{1}{10}$ l.) sour cream, 2½–5 tsp. olive oil, juice of 1–1½ lemons, salt, pinch of sugar.

Wash and drain lettuce and tear into strips. Cut carrot into strips and the orange and pineapple into pieces. For the dressing, combine the sour cream with the oil and season with lemon juice, salt and sugar. Pour over the salad. Serve with slices of toast or fried potatoes.

Basle Apples
(BASLER ÄPFELTELLER)

Ingredients: 5 apples, little butter, sugar, 5½ oz. (150 g.) mayonnaise, 1 oz. (30 g.) shredded hazelnuts, lemon juice.

Peel and core the apples, cut one into four slices and dice the others. Drip a little melted butter onto the apple slices, coat with sugar and place on a baking sheet. Put into a medium hot oven and bake until golden brown. Meanwhile flavour the mayonnaise with the lemon juice and mix with the diced apples and hazelnuts. Arrange the salad on a dish and surround with the apple slices when cool. Alternatively, arrange on individual plates and decorate each with one slice.

Can be served as a first course or as a side dish with the meat course.

Apple Slices Florida
(APFELSCHEIBEN FLORIDA)

Ingredients: 2 apples, 1 glass white wine, 1¾ tsp. sugar, 2 cloves, ½ cooked celeriac or 2 sticks celery, 1–2 pineapple rings, 4½ oz. (125 g.) mayonnaise, juice of 1 lemon, salt, pepper, lettuce or red pepper or stuffed olives.

Peel and core the apples, cut into slices, place in a pan with the wine, sugar and cloves and poach for a short time. They should not be too soft. Drain and leave to cool. In the meantime shred or dice the pineapple and celery, season the mayonnaise with lemon juice, pepper and salt and mix. Place the apple slices on a dish, pile the salad on top and leave for an hour before serving. Shredded lettuce, strips of tinned red pepper or stuffed olives can be used as garnish.

Stuffed Tomatoes Monte Carlo
(GEFÜLLTE TOMATEN À LA MONTE CARLO)

Ingredients: 4 tomatoes, 3 pineapple rings, 2 figs, mayonnaise, little condensed milk, tomato ketchup, lettuce leaves.

Cut the top off the tomatoes and scoop out flesh. Chop the figs and pineapple very small and mix with the mayonnaise thinned with condensed milk, to which ketchup has been added. Stuff the tomatoes with the mixture, replace the tops and decorate with tiny blobs of mayonnaise. Serve on a bed of lettuce. Hand round bread or toast.

Apple Slices Dolores
(APFELSCHEIBEN DOLORES)

Ingredients: 3 cooking apples, 3 2-oz. (60 g.) pkt. Gervaise demi-sel or ½ lb. (250 g.) cream cheese, paprika, butter, lettuce leaves.

Peel the apples, remove the cores and cut into slices. Cream the cheese with butter and season with paprika. Spread the apple slices with this mixture, arrange on lettuce and serve with toast or pumpernickel.

Suitable as a first course or as an intermediate course in a festive meal.

Stuffed Pears
(GEFÜLLTE BIRNENHÄLFTEN)

Ingredients: 4 pears, ½ lb. (250 g.) curd cheese, ¾–1½ tbsp. condensed milk, 1½ tbsp. lemon juice, 2 oz. (65 g.) sugar, 1½ oz. (50 g.) grated hazelnuts or almonds, 4 whole nuts or cherries.

Peel the pears and scoop out the interiors. Leave raw or poach lightly. If raw pears are used, sprinkle them with lemon juice and let it soak in to preserve whiteness. Cream the cheese with the milk and gradually add the lemon juice, sugar and grated nuts. Stuff the pears with the cheese cream and decorate each with a hazelnut, almond or a fresh or candied cherry.

For a savoury stuffing, mix the curd cheese with tomato purée and paprika or with finely chopped herbs and serve on a bed of lettuce leaves.

Stuffed Oranges
(GEFÜLLTE ORANGENHÄLFTEN)

Ingredients: 3–4 oranges, cooked celery, 1–2 cooking apples, mayonnaise, condensed milk, handful of chopped nuts, rind of 1 orange, sugar, water.

Cut the orange in half, remove the pulp carefully and pink the edges with scissors or a sharp knife. Chop the pulp together with the peeled apples and celery and mix with the mayonnaise thinned with condensed milk. Pile the salad into the orange shells. Candy the orange rind by cutting into thin strips and cooking in a sugar-and-water syrup. Garnish salad with candied rind and chopped nuts.

The orange baskets can be stuffed with any other fruit salad or filled with cream. They are always attractive.

Fruit Salad Bama
(FRUCHT-SALAT BAMA)

Ingredients per person: ½ grapefruit, 1 banana, ½ orange, sugar,
cherry or ½ walnut or orange slice.

Cut the grapefruit in half. Remove the flesh carefully with a
small silver spoon, cut it into small pieces together with the
peeled banana and orange. Mix well together and add sugar
if desired. Pile the salad into the grapefruit shells and decorate
each with a slice of orange, a cherry or half a walnut.

Winter Hors d'Oeuvre
(WINTERLICHES VORGERICHT)

Ingredients: 2 grapefruit, 2–3 pineapple rings, 1 orange, sugar,
3½ tbsp. grated hazelnuts or almonds, 4 fl. oz.
($\frac{1}{10}$ l.) yogurt or sour cream, 1–2 walnuts.

Halve the grapefruit, scoop out the flesh and remove the pith.
Peel the orange and cut all the fruit into small pieces. Mix, add
the sugar and hazelnuts or almonds and pile into the grapefruit halves. Top each with a tablespoonful of cream or
yogurt and garnish with half a walnut.

This salad can be served as an accompaniment with meat
dishes, in which case the nuts should be omitted.

Stuffed Grapefruit
(GEFÜLLTE GRAPEFRUITHÄLFTEN)

Ingredients: 2 grapefruit, 2 apples, ½ celeriac or 2 sticks celery,
salad oil, vinegar, pinch of sugar, salt.

Halve the grapefruit, scoop out the flesh and chop. Shred the
peeled and cored apples and the celery. Mix, dress with the
oil, vinegar, salt and sugar and pile into grapefruit halves.

Delicious as a first course or with game.

Cauliflower Salad
(BLUMENKOHLSALAT)

Ingredients: 1 small cauliflower, 1½ tbsp. blanched and
shredded almonds, 1½ tbsp. raisins, ¼ pt. (⅛ l.) sour
cream, juice of 1–2 lemons, lettuce leaves.

Trim, wash and break the cauliflower into flowerets. Poach in salted water for a few minutes. Mix the dressing and add almonds and raisins.

Serve on lettuce leaves with toast as a first course, or as a side dish with game or poultry.

Salad Miami
(SALAT MIAMI)

Ingredients: 2 oranges, 4 pineapple rings, 1 small cooked cauliflower, 3½ oz. (100 g.) mayonnaise, milk, tomato
ketchup.

Peel the oranges. Separate the cauliflower into flowerets. Chop the fruit and add to the cauliflower. Thin the mayonnaise with a little milk and flavour with ketchup. Pour over the salad mixture.

Serve on slices of toast as a first course or to accompany game or poultry. In the latter case the amounts may have to be increased.

Salad Natasha
(SALAT NATASCHA)

Ingredients: 1 cucumber, 1 orange, 1 tbsp. grated hazelnuts,
¼ pt. (⅛ l.) sour cream, juice of 1 lemon, salt,
pepper, paprika, sugar.

Peel and slice the cucumber and orange and arrange the slices overlapping on a plate. Sprinkle with hazelnuts. Season the cream, adding a pinch of sugar, if desired, and pour over the salad.

Grilled Fruit Salad Lucullus
(OBSTSALAT LUKULL GEGRILLT)

Ingredients: 1½ lb. (500–750 g.) mixed fruit (apples, pears,
oranges, pineapple, peaches, apricots), 1½–2 oz.
(50 g.) raisins, 1 pkt. (1½ tbsp.) vanilla sugar,
sugar, brandy or rum.

Peel and prepare the fruit and cut into small pieces. Add vanilla sugar with a little additional sugar and pour the brandy over the salad. Cut 4 to 5 squares from aluminium foil and butter on one side. Divide the salad into the same number of portions, place portions on squares and bend foil around the salad to form parcels. Seal round the edges and place under the hot grill for a few minutes. Open top of foil and serve hot.

COMBINATION SALADS AND COCKTAILS

Fruit and Vegetable Salad
(KOMBINIERTER OBST-GEMÜSE-SALAT)

Ingredients: 1 cauliflower, 1 orange, 1–2 pineapple rings, 4 slices smoked tongue, 1–2 tomatoes, 4½ oz. (125 g.) mayonnaise, tinned milk, salt, juice of ½ lemon, lettuce leaves, strips of red pepper.

Trim the cauliflower, break into flowerets and poach in salted water for about 5 minutes. Drain. Cut the peeled orange, pineapple, tomatoes and tongue into small pieces. Mix the salad. Thin the mayonnaise with the tinned milk, season to taste and pour over. Serve on a bed of lettuce leaves and garnish with strips of red peppers.

Alternatively, shape the tongue slices into cones and fill with the other salad ingredients mixed with the thinned mayonnaise.

Cocktail Sanssouci

Ingredients: 7 oz. (200 g.) cooked chicken or game, 2 pineapple rings, 12 blanched and shredded almonds, little mayonnaise, milk, tomato ketchup, juice of 1–2 oranges or lemons, paprika.

Cut the meat and pineapple into small pieces. Thin the mayonnaise with a little milk, flavour with fruit juice and ketchup and combine the salad. Serve on small plates. Sprinkle with paprika if desired, and hand round small fresh rolls and butter.

Salad à la Provence

Ingredients: Chicken leftovers, 1 banana, 2 pineapple rings, 3½ oz. (100 g.) fresh or tinned mushrooms, mayonnaise, tomato ketchup, ½ tsp. French mustard, juice of 1–2 lemons.

Dice the meat, pineapple and banana. Wash, slice and cook fresh mushrooms in a little butter for a few minutes, slice or halve tinned ones. Add to the salad. Flavour the mayonnaise with remaining ingredients and combine with the salad mixture. Serve with bread or toast.

Viennese Meat Salad
(WIENER FLEISCHSALAT)

Ingredients: 7 oz. (200 g.) cooked beef, 1 head chicory, 1 apple, 1 orange, 7–8 tbsp. yogurt, juice of ½ lemon, salt, pinch of sugar.

Trim and slice the chicory thinly. Dice the beef and the peeled apple and orange. Whisk the yogurt, season with remaining ingredients and combine the salad.

Chicken or turkey leftovers may be used instead of beef.

Tuna Cocktail Renate
(THUNFISCH-COCKTAIL RENATE)

Ingredients: ½ grapefruit, 2 small or 1 medium tin tuna, mayonnaise, tinned milk, tomato ketchup.

Peel and dice the grapefruit. Add the shredded tuna. Thin the mayonnaise with a little tinned milk and flavour with ketchup. Arrange the salad in cocktail cups and pour the mayonnaise over. Serve chilled with slices of toast.

This delicious salad is almost equal to lobster cocktail in flavour and far less expensive.

Crab Heligoland
(HELIGOLÄNDER KRABBENSPEISE)

Ingredients: 2 juicy apples, 7 oz. (200 g.) cooked crabmeat, ¼ pt. (⅛ l.) double cream, 1½–2 tbsp. mayonnaise, olives.

Peel and core the apples, and cut into thick slices. Soak the crabmeat in a little water, drain and arrange on the apple slices. Mix cream with the mayonnaise and put this on top of the meat. Decorate each portion with an olive.

Alternatively, the apples can be diced and mixed with the crab and dressing. Arrange on lettuce leaves or slices of toast.

For the dressing, the cream may be omitted by using mayonnaise flavoured with lemon juice and tomato ketchup instead.

Stuffed Apples – Russian Style.
(GEFÜLLTE ÄPFEL AUF RUSSISCHE ART)

Ingredients: 4–6 large apples, 4 oz. (100–125 g.) cooked meat, 3½ oz. (100 g.) ham, 1–2 anchovy fillets, 4½ oz. (125 g.) cooked celery, 2 hard-boiled eggs, 1 sour gherkin, French mustard, paprika, capers, mayonnaise, 1 tomato, parsley.

Peel the apples and scoop out the interior, leaving a wall about ¾ inch thick. Dice the meats, anchovies, eggs, celery, gherkin and the inside of the apple. Mix with the mayonnaise and season well with capers, mustard and paprika. Stuff the apples with the mixture, decorate each with a tomato slice and leave for 1 hour. Arrange on a bed of parsley and serve.

Melon Hors d'Oeuvre
(MELONE ALS HORS D'OEUVRE)

Ingredients per person: 2 oz. (50 g.) finely sliced ham or any smoked continental meat available in delicatessen shops, piece of melon, lettuce leaves, mayonnaise.

Arrange the slices of meat on lettuce leaves, together with slices of well chilled melon from which the pips have been removed. The meat can be garnished with a spoonful of mayonnaise if desired.

Posen Melon Slices
(POSENER MELONENSCHNITZE)

Ingredients: 4 thick slices melon, 4 large slices lean ham, lettuce leaves, juice of 2 lemons, 4 fl. oz. ($\frac{1}{10}$ l.) sour cream, paprika.

Remove pips from the melon slices, chill, arrange on lettuce leaves and pour over a dressing made by mixing the lemon juice and cream. Chop up the ham and garnish the lettuce leaves with it. Dust with paprika if desired and serve with slices of bread or toast.

Bananas à la Marlene
(BANANEN À LA MARLENE)

Ingredients: 2 bananas, 5½ oz. (150 g.) cooked meat, salt, pepper, piece of lemon, 4 fl. oz. ($\frac{1}{10}$ l.) sour cream, 4 slices toast.

Slice the bananas and meat. Make the dressing from cream and seasonings, mix everything well and serve on toast.

Ragout of Bananas
(BANANENRAGOUT)

Ingredients: 4–5 bananas, 3½ oz. (100 g.) cooked gammon or lean ham, fat, salt, 3½ tbsp. fine white breadcrumbs, 1 oz. (30 g.) butter.

Slice the bananas and mix with the chopped meat. Grease 4 individual heatproof pots or cocottes, add a pinch of salt and fill with the mixture. Sprinkle with crumbs, dot with butter and bake in a moderate oven for 10 minutes.

Banana au Gratin
(GRATINIERTE BANANEN)

Ingredients: 3–4 tomatoes, 5½ oz. (150 g.) minced beef, salt, basil, nutmeg, fat, 1 banana, 3½–5 tbsp. grated Gruyère cheese, butter.

Slice the tomatoes. Season the meat with salt, basil and nutmeg. Melt a little fat in a pan and fry the meat for a few minutes adding a little water. Butter a shallow heatproof dish, arrange half the tomatoes to cover the bottom of the dish. Put in the meat mixture and top with the rest of the tomatoes. Slice the banana and distribute over the dish. Sprinkle the cheese on top, dot with butter and bake for 10 minutes in a moderate oven. When the cheese is turning golden put under the hot grill for a short time, then serve immediately.

Fruit to Accompany
Meat Dishes

Whatever is served with meat, be it fruit or vegetables, should
be served in small portions. Its function is twofold: to please
the eye and thereby stimulate the appetite, and to add flavour
to the meal. The following recipes can be used all the year
round, with frozen fruits replacing fresh ones out of season.

Cherry Istanbul
(KIRSCHGEMÜSE STAMBUL)

Ingredients: ½ lb. (250 g.) cherries, sugar, 1 oz. (30 g.) butter,
1¼ tbsp. flour, lemon juice.

Wash and stone the cherries, put into a pan with ½ pint (¼
litre) water, sugar to taste and cook until tender. Drain and
reserve the syrup. In a separate pan make a roux with the
butter and flour, stir in the syrup, simmer until it thickens then
add the cherries. Flavour with lemon juice.

This cherry dish tastes delicious with game or steak.

Spiced Peaches in Butter
(GEWÜRZPFIRSICHE IN BUTTER GEBACKEN)

Ingredients: 2–4 large peaches, a few cloves, 1 pkt. (1½ tbsp.) vanilla sugar, 2–3 tbsp. sugar, butter.

Wash and halve the peaches, remove the stones and stud each half with 2–3 cloves. Place the halves in a buttered heatproof dish and sprinkle with vanilla sugar and sugar. Cover with a lid or aluminium foil and bake in a moderate oven for 10 minutes.

This goes well with rice or meat dishes.

Grilled Peaches
(GEGRILLTE PFIRSICHE)

Ingredients: 2–4 large peaches, 4 slices ham, 2–4 slices Cheshire cheese.

Plunge the peaches into hot water for a few moments and skin. Halve, remove stones and wrap half a slice of ham around each piece of fruit. Place a piece of cheese on top and secure with a cocktail stick. Put under a hot grill until the cheese begins to bubble and serve at once.

This is excellent with all kinds of meat or poultry, but can also be served as a snack on its own with bread and butter.

Cranberries and Pears
(PREISELBEERSCHÜSSEL)

Ingredients: ½ lb. (250 g.) sugar, 1–1½ lb. (500–750 g.) pears, ½–1 lb. (250–500 g.) cranberries, 1 stick cinnamon, 1 pkt. (1½ tbsp.) vanilla sugar.

Peel and cut the pears into small pieces. Bring 1¾ pints (1 litre) water to the boil with the sugar. Add the pears and cook until nearly soft. Wash and clean the cranberries, add them to the pears with the cinnamon and continue to cook until the berries are quite soft. Remove the cinnamon and add the vanilla sugar.

Serve hot or cold with soufflés, pancakes, dumplings or puddings.

Cranberry Compote Lucullus
(PREISELBEERKOMPOTT)

Ingredients: Cranberry compote, chopped hazelnuts, 1 orange.

Peel and chop the orange. Combine ingredients.
  Serve with game, steak or white meats.

Anklam Plum Dish
(ANKLAMER ZWETSCHGENSCHÜSSEL)

Ingredients: 1 lb. (500 g.) plums, rind of $\frac{1}{2}$ lemon, sugar, $1\frac{1}{2}$ oz.
                (40 g.) butter or margarine, 2 oz. (60 g.) flour, salt,
                vinegar.

Wash the plums, stone and cook with sugar and the lemon
rind in water until nearly soft but not mushy. Drain, remove
lemon rind and reserve the juice. Make a roux from the butter
and flour, stir in the plum juice, season with a pinch of salt
and finally add the fruit. Add a few drops of vinegar to give a
sweet-sour taste.
  Particularly good as an accompaniment to boiled beef.

Plum Salad Malakoff
(ZWETSCHGENSALAT MALAKOFF)

Ingredients: 1 lb. (500 g.) plums, 8 fl. oz. ($\frac{1}{5}$ l.) sour cream,
                lemon juice, lettuce.

Wash, stone and chop the plums. Arrange the fruit on a bed of
shredded lettuce, stir lemon juice into the cream and pour over.

Pear Slices Carol
(BIRNENSCHNITZE CAROL)

Ingredients: 1–1$\frac{3}{4}$ lb. (500–750 g.) pears, 2–2$\frac{1}{2}$ oz. (65 g.) butter,
                3$\frac{1}{2}$ tbsp. sugar.

Peel, quarter and core the pears. Melt the butter in a pan over
a low heat, add half the sugar and the pears and cook them
gently in their own juice if possible. The fruit turns brown
just before it is done. Sprinkle the rest of the sugar on top.
  Serve with game or poultry dishes.

Pears in Brown Sauce
(BIRNEN IN BRAUNER SAUCE)

Ingredients: 3 large pears, 1 pt. ($\frac{1}{2}$ l.) clear soup or beef cube
dissolved in water, 2 oz. (60 g.) margarine, 5 oz.
(140 g.) flour, salt, vinegar.

Peel the pears and cook whole in the soup until tender. Drain
on a sieve, quarter and remove the cores. Make a roux from
the margarine and flour, cook until well browned and add the
soup made up to 1 pint ($\frac{1}{2}$ litre). Return the fruit to the sauce
and flavour with salt and vinegar.

Serve with boiled beef and potato dumplings.

Savoury Melons
(PIKANTES MELONENGEMÜSE)

Ingredients: 1 medium-sized melon, 4 oz. (100 g.) bacon,
1 green pepper, 1 onion, salt, curry powder,
tomato ketchup.

Quarter the melon, discard the pips, carefully remove the
flesh and dice. Chop the bacon and the onion. Remove
the top of the pepper, its seeds and white parts, and cut the
flesh into thin strips. Put the bacon and onion into a frying
pan and cook gently until the onion turns transparent, then
add the pepper and melon. Continue to cook until all the
vegetables are done. Season with salt and curry powder,
arrange on a dish and serve with grated cheese.

Italian Bananas
(ITALIENISCHES BANANENGEMÜSE)

Ingredients: 1–2 onions, 1$\frac{1}{2}$ oz. (40 g.) butter, 3–4 bananas,
3–4 tomatoes, salt, lemon juice or white wine.

Chop the onions finely and cook gently in the butter. Peel the
tomatoes by plunging them into hot water for a few moments,
after which the skin comes away easily, and chop. Slice the
bananas. Cook everything for 8–10 minutes and season with
salt and lemon juice or wine.

Fried Bananas
(GEBACKENE BANANENHÄLFTEN)

Ingredients: 2–3 bananas, lemon juice, 1 pkt. (1½ tbsp.) vanilla
sugar, 1–2 egg yolks, fine breadcrumbs, fat, horseradish, 4 fl. oz. ($\frac{1}{10}$ l.) double cream.

Peel the bananas and cut into slices lengthwise. Sprinkle with
lemon juice and vanilla sugar and coat with beaten egg and
breadcrumbs. Heat fat in a pan and fry the banana slices very
quickly on both sides. They are done in a few moments. Lift
carefully on to a serving dish and arrange the mixed cream and
horseradish on top.

Fried banana slices can be served as a sweet course, in which
case they should be garnished with thick gooseberry compote
instead of horseradish.

Bananas in a Jacket
(BANANEN IM ROCK)

Ingredients: 2 bananas, 1 egg yolk, 2½ tsp. lemon juice, 6–7
tbsp. breadcrumbs, fat, lettuce leaves.

Peel and halve the bananas. Beat the yolk with the lemon
juice and brush the fruit with it. Coat with breadcrumbs and
fry in deep fat until crisp. Arrange on lettuce.

Serve as a side dish with meat.

Indian Bananas
(INDIAN BANANENSPEISE)

Ingredients: 2–3 bananas, 3 tomatoes, ½ pt. (¼ l.) white wine,
salt, sugar, pinch of nutmeg.

Skin the tomatoes, peel the bananas, slice and place the fruit
in a dish. Add seasonings to the wine, pour over and leave for
20 minutes. Lift the fruit out of the marinade.

Serve as a side dish with meat.

Apple as a Vegetable
(APFELGEMÜSE)

Ingredients: 1 lb. (500 g.) apples, 1½ oz. (50 g.) raisins, piece
of butter, white wine, juice of ½ lemon.

Peel, core and slice the apples. Cook in a little water until tender and add the raisins which have been washed and soaked in water. Finally, stir in the butter and flavour with wine and lemon juice.

Delicious with roast duck or goose, or with game.

Apple Creole
(KREOLISCHES APFELGEMÜSE)

Ingredients: 1¾ lb. (750 g.) apples, juice of 1 lemon, 1 onion, fat, sugar, salt.

Peel, core and chop the apples and sprinkle with lemon juice. Slice the onion finely and cook gently in fat until transparent. Add the chopped apples and continue to cook until they are tender but not mushy. Season with sugar and a pinch of salt.

Curry powder can be added if desired, in which case the sugar should be omitted.

Serve with rice.

Hungarian Apple Salad
(UNGARISCHER APFELSALAT)

Ingredients: 4–5 large cooked potatoes, 2 apples, ½ onion, 3–4 tbsp. olive oil, 2 tbsp. vinegar, salt.

Peel the apples, dice or slice together with the potatoes. Grate the onion. Make the dressing of oil, vinegar and salt and mix the salad well. If it appears too dry, add 1½ tablespoons beef bouillon.

Serve with roast pork.

Red Apple Salad
(ROTER APFELSALAT)

Ingredients: 2–3 apples, 1 raw beetroot, grated horseradish, oil, vinegar, salt, pinch of sugar.

Peel and grate the apples and beetroot and mix together. Make the dressing and add, together with plenty of horseradish.

Excellent with game or poultry, or with cold meat.

Apple Salad à la Romaine
(APFELSALAT À LA ROMAINE)

Ingredients: 3 large apples, 2–3 oz. (50–100 g.) Gruyère cheese, 2–3 oz. (50–100 g.) mustard and cress, pinch of salt, vinegar, oil.

Peel, core and dice the apples. Dice the cheese, mix with the apples and pile into a serving dish. Make the dressing, pour over the salad and garnish with cress.

Good with cold or hot meat dishes.

Apple Cream
(APFELCREME)

Ingredients: ¾ lb. (375 g.) curd cheese, 2½ tbsp. milk, 1–2 small onions, 1 large or 2 small apples, 1 tbsp. tomato purée, chives.

Blend the milk with the cheese and beat well. Peel and grate the apples, dice the onions finely and chop the chives. Mix everything well together.

Serve with fried potatoes, Italian pasta dishes or pies.

Apple Horseradish Cream
(APFEL-MEERRETTICH-CREME)

Ingredients: 1–2 apples, ¾ tsp. vinegar or lemon juice, 3½ tbsp. grated horseradish, ¼–½ pt. (⅛–¼ litre) cream or apple juice, sugar.

Peel, core and grate the apples and mix with lemon juice or vinegar to keep them white. Combine with the rest of the ingredients, adding sugar to taste.

Condensed milk can be substituted for the cream or apple juice.

Serve with beef, game or poultry.

Grilled Apples
(ÄPFEL-GRILLTELLER)

Ingredients: 4 juicy apples, 7–10 tbsp. raisins, butter, 2½–5 tsp. white wine per apple.

Peel the apples, carefully remove the cores and stuff with the

63

raisins. From aluminium foil cut 4 squares of a suitable size and butter them on one side. Place one apple on each square and wrap around the fruit. Before sealing the top pour the wine over the fruit and a little sugar mixed with vanilla sugar if desired. Seal and place under the hot grill for a few minutes. Cut or tear the foil open in the shape of a leaf and serve.

Instead of raisins, the same amount of cranberry jam or fruit steeped in rum can be used, and brandy, rum or port used instead of white wine.

As an alternative method, slice the apples, spread with butter and grill. Sprinkle the slices with brandy and serve in a raisin sauce with white meats or as a sweet dish.

Sliced pears or halved apricots or peaches may be grilled in the same way. These should be served in a wine sauce or custard.

Stuffed Apples 1
(GEFÜLLTE ÄPFEL)

Ingredients: 4 large cooking apples, 4 oz. (100 g.) pig's liver, 1 oz. (30 g.) bacon, salt, oregano, butter, white wine.

Peel the apples, remove the core and a little of the flesh to create a space for the stuffing. Mince or chop the liver and bacon finely, season with salt and oregano, stuff the apples with the mixture and place them in a buttered heatproof dish. Add a little water or wine and bake in a moderate oven for 20 minutes.

Stuffed Apples 2

Ingredients: 4 large cooking apples, cooked red cabbage, butter, white wine.

Stuff the apples with the cabbage, to which a little grated apple has been added, and bake as above.

Apples Stuffed with Cranberries
(ÄPFEL MIT PREISELBEERKOMPOTT GEFÜLLT)

Ingredients: 4 medium-sized apples, cranberry compote.

Peel and core the apples and poach for a short time in water or wine, taking care not to overcook them. Lift out the apples with a spoon and stuff while still hot with cranberries. Red-currant jelly can be used similarly to cranberries.

These apples taste delicious served with game or poultry dishes, soup or white meats. Alternatively, serve with custard as a dessert.

Devilled Oranges Anatol
(TEUFELSSCHEIBEN ANATOL)

Ingredients per person: 2 orange slices, 2 thin onion slices, olive oil, olives, paprika.

Fry the onions gently in a little oil. Place the orange slices on a dish, top each with an onion slice and secure with a cocktail stick. Sprinkle paprika on top and garnish with sliced olives.

Serve with game, poultry or meat dishes. This exotic delicacy is highly valued by Turkish gourmets.

Orange Salad
(ORANGENSALAT)

Ingredients: 1 lb. (500 g.) oranges, 1 apple, sugar, $\frac{1}{4}$–$\frac{1}{2}$ pt. ($\frac{1}{4}$ l.) white wine or apple juice.

Peel and core the apple, peel oranges and remove the pith. Chop all the fruit, place in dishes and sprinkle with sugar to taste. Pour over wine or juice and leave for 1 hour.

Serve with meat or as a refreshing dessert.

Oranges in Wine
(ORANGENSCHEIBEN IN WEISSWEIN)

Ingredients: 1–2 oranges, sugar, white wine.

Peel the oranges, remove pith and slice thinly. Add a little sugar and enough wine to cover.

Use as a garnish for roast duck, chicken or turkey, or serve on a separate plate as a side dish.

Waldorf Salad
(Original Recipe)
(SALADE WALDORF)

Ingredients: 3 ripe apples, 1½ oz. (40 g.) chopped walnuts, 1 lettuce heart, 2–3 sticks celery or 1 cooked celeriac, thick mayonnaise, mustard, paprika.

Peel, core and dice the apples. Wash and shred the lettuce. Slice celery or celeriac very finely. Season mayonnaise with mustard and paprika and combine the salad, adding the chopped walnuts. Serve chilled.

Salad Mikado
(SALAT MIKADO)

Ingredients: 7 oz. (200 g.) rice, 7 oz. (200 g.) cooked meat, 1 apple, 1 banana, 3 anchovy fillets, 5–7 oz. (150–200 g.) mayonnaise, paprika, pepper, lemon juice.

Cook the rice in fast boiling water for 12 minutes, drain, spray with cold water and leave to cool. Chop the meat, peeled apple, banana and anchovies finely and mix with the rice. Mix in the seasoned mayonnaise. Chill and serve with a salad of endives or cress.

Kombi Salad
(KOMBI SALAT)

Ingredients: ½ lb. (250 g.) redcurrants, 2 grated apples, 2 grated carrots, ½ pt. (¼ l.) sour cream, juice of ½ lemon, sugar.

Clean and wash the currants and drain on a sieve. Sprinkle the grated apple with lemon juice to prevent discoloration. Mix all the ingredients well. Serve sugar separately.

Brazil Salad
(PARA-SALAT)

Ingredients: 2 pineapple rings, 1 small cooked celeriac or 1 stick celery, 2 oz. (50 g.) grapes, 1 apple, juice of ½ lemon, 10 shelled Brazil nuts, 4½ oz. (125 g.) mayonnaise, condensed milk, salt, paprika.

Dice the pineapple, celery and the peeled apple. Sprinkle with lemon juice. Add the grapes and finely chopped nuts. Thin the mayonnaise with milk, season with salt and paprika and combine the salad. Chill.

Serve with roasts.

Sauerkraut Salad with Fruit
(SAUERKRAUT-ROHKOST-SALAT MIT OBST)

Ingredients: 10½ oz. (300 g.) sauerkraut, 1 apple, 2 pineapple rings, ¼ pt. (⅛ l.) sour cream, ¾ tsp. tomato ketchup.

Loosen the sauerkraut with a fork and chop very finely. Peel the apple. Shred apple and pineapple. Mix sauerkraut with the fruit and combine with cream and ketchup.

This salad is more easily digested if the sauerkraut is first pounded lightly before it is added to the salad.

Swedish Coleslaw
(SCHWEDISCHER WEISSKRAUTSALAT)

Ingredients: 1 small head of white cabbage, 3 carrots, 1–2 peeled apples, ¼ pt. (⅛ l.) sour cream, 2½ tsp. vinegar or juice of 2 lemons, salt, pinch of sugar.

Quarter the cabbage and shred finely. Add grated apples and carrots. Mix the dressing and combine the salad.

Thin mayonnaise may be used instead of the cream dressing.

Silesian Turnips
(TELTOWER RÜBCHEN AUF SCHLESISCHE ART)

Ingredients: 1 lb. (500 g.) small, young turnips, salt, pinch of sugar, butter, flour, 1½ tbsp. sultanas.

Peel the turnips, leave them whole and cook until tender in water to which sugar, salt and sultanas have been added. Drain. Make a roux with the butter and flour, add a little of the liquid and finally the turnips.

The flavour can be improved by the addition of a few slices of apple, previously fried in butter.

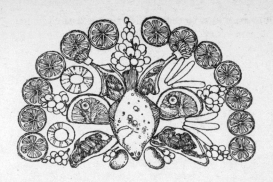

Main Course Dishes with Fruit

It has become the custom in the United States to serve meat with a garnish of pineapple, peaches or other fruit. Rich meats as well as grilled dishes become more digestible when eaten with fruit. In addition, many meat, fish and vegetable dishes acquire an exotic note through the addition of fruit, both visually and flavourwise. It is the contrast that achieves the effect.

MEAT WITH FRUIT

Pork with Apples à la Hagen
(HAGENER FLEISCH-GERICHT MIT ÄPFEL)

Ingredients: ¾–1 lb. (375–500 g.) pork (not too lean), fat, 2 onions, ¼–½ pt. (¼ l.) cooking wine (white), 2–3 apples, flour, salt, juice of 1 lemon.

Slice the onion finely, dice the pork, peel and dice the apples. Heat fat in a pan, put in the meat and onions and fry until brown. Add the apples and the wine, cover and simmer gently for about 45 minutes. Thicken the gravy with flour, flavour with lemon juice and adjust seasoning.

Yogurt may be added to the finished dish if desired. This, however, must be added off the heat as boiling would destroy all the goodness.

Liver – Berlin Style
(BERLINER LEBER)

Ingredients: 14 oz. (400 g.) liver (calf or ox), flour, fat, 1–2 onions, salt, pepper, marjoram, 1–2 cooking apples, white wine.

Wash and slice the liver, coat with flour and fry quickly in hot fat. Season with salt and pepper and a little marjoram, if desired. Lift on to a serving dish. Peel the apples and onions, slice and fry in the fat. Sprinkle wine over the apples and arrange the onion and apple slices with the liver.

Liver – Swiss Style
(LEBER AUF SCHWEIZER ART)

Ingredients: 14 oz. (400 g.) liver (calf or ox), flour, fat, 1–2 onions, salt, pepper, marjoram, 1–2 cooking apples, lemon juice.

Cut the liver into thin strips, flour, and fry quickly in fat. Peel and chop the onions, peel and slice the apples, fry both separately in fat, season and sprinkle with lemon juice.

Yet another version from the Alsace: fry the liver and serve on fried banana slices.

Beefsteak Montevideo

Ingredients: ¾ lb. (375 g.) minced meat (beef, veal, pork or a mixture), 2 large onions, parsley, 1–2 rolls, 1 egg, salt, pepper, nutmeg, fine breadcrumbs, fat, 1–2 apples, 1½ tbsp. sugar.

Place the meat into a mixing bowl and add 1 minced or chopped onion. Soak the rolls in a little water, squeeze out surplus liquid and mince or break up with a fork. Add to the mixture together with the beaten egg, chopped parsley and seasonings.

Work everything together and form cakes. Coat with breadcrumbs and fry in hot fat until nicely browned and crisp on the outside. Peel the apples and slice thickly, slice the second onion. Heat fat, add the sugar and fry the apples and onions until golden. Arrange the meatballs on a dish and place a slice of onion and apple on each.

Alternatively, place sliced bananas on the meatballs and grill just before serving.

Silesian Paradise
(SCHLESISCHES HIMMELREICH)

Ingredients: ¾ lb. (375 g.) pork, fat, ½ lb. (250 g.) mixed dried fruit, salt, pinch of sugar, ground cloves, cinnamon, flour.

Soak the fruit in water for an hour. Wash the meat, cut into small pieces, sprinkle with salt and fry in hot fat until crisp. Add a little water, cover the pan and cook until nearly done. Drain the fruit, add to the meat and cook until tender. Season, adding a pinch of cinnamon and thickening the gravy with flour if desired. Serve with dumplings.

Kassell Chops with Mandarins
(KASSELER RIPPESPEER MIT MANDARINEN)

Ingredients: 4 smoked pork chops, salt, pepper, 2 cloves, 2–3 tsp. potato flour, 4 fl. oz. ($\frac{1}{10}$ l.) sour cream, 1 small tin mandarin oranges.

Put the meat in a pan with a scant ½ pint (¼ litre) water seasoned with salt, pepper and cloves. Bring to the boil. Transfer meat and water to a heatproof dish, add syrup from the mandarins and cook until the meat is tender, basting frequently. It should take about 1 hour. Lift the chops on to a serving dish, thicken the gravy with potato flour, add the cream and adjust seasoning. Pour a little of the gravy over the meat, decorate with mandarin orange sections. Serve with boiled rice or potato purée and hand the rest of the gravy round separately.

Syrian Rice Dish
(SYRISCHES REISGERICHT)

Ingredients: 7 oz. (200 g.) rice, 4 oz. (125 g.) each of finely
chopped or minced veal and beef, salt, fat, 1 onion,
1 apple, 1½ tsp. curry powder, 3 tbsp. raisins, 1½
figs, 1 banana.

Wash the rice and bring to the boil in salted water. Drain and
put into fresh water with a little salt. Cook for 10–15 minutes.
Drain, spray with cold water, then keep the rice warm.

Peel and chop the apple and onion, wash the raisins, chop
the figs and slice the banana. Fry the meat with the onion in
hot fat, then add all the fruit together with 1 pint (½ litre)
water or stock and the curry powder and cook for 12–15
minutes. Serve mixed with the rice, on a bed of rice or hand the
rice separately.

Mincemeat Quickie
(SCHNELLGERICHT GESCHNETZELTES)

Ingredients: ¾ lb. (375 g.) minced pork or veal, 1½–2 oz. (40–
60 g.) fat, curry powder, 1 onion, 1–2 cooking
apples, ¾–1 pt. (½ l.) beef stock, ¼ oz. (10 g.)
potato flour, salt.

Chop the onion and fry in hot fat. Add the meat, dust with
curry powder and brown all over. Pour the stock over and
cook for about 10 minutes. Remove the meat from the gravy,
thicken with potato flour and season. Arrange the meat with
the gravy and garnish with apple slices fried in fat. Serve with
curry rice.

Roast Pork Charlotte
(SCHWEINEBRATEN CHARLOTTE)

Ingredients: 1 lb. (500 g.) belly pork, salt, pepper, ½ lb. (250 g.)
cooking apples, 1 tbsp. grated ryebread or soft
white breadcrumbs, 2 cloves, fat, flour.

Ask the butcher to cut a pocket in the meat. Make a stuffing
with the chopped apples and bread, rub the meat with salt and

pepper, fill the pocket tightly and sew up the opening with needle and thread. Insert the cloves and brown the meat on both sides in hot fat. Add a little water and roast until tender. Lift the meat out, thicken the gravy with flour, strain if necessary and adjust seasoning. Remove thread. Serve the gravy separately.

Danish Pork with Apples
(DÄNISCHER SCHWEINEBRATEN MIT OBST GESPICKT)

Ingredients: 1½ lb. (500–750 g.) belly pork, 2–3 apples, salt, pepper, 1 onion, fat, 4 fl. oz. ($\frac{1}{10}$ l.) sour cream, flour.

Bone the meat and with a sharp knife make a number of slits on the inner side. Halve and core the apples and cut into slices. Insert the apple slices into the slits, season with pepper and salt. Place in hot fat together with the chopped onion and brown on both sides. Add water, cover and cook until done. Finally, add the sour cream and thicken with flour if desired. In Denmark, small baked potatoes or potato crisps are served with the pork.

For a variation, use 5 ounces (125–150 grammes) prunes instead of apples.

Beef Curry à l'Anglaise
(RINDS-CURRY AUF ENGLISCHE ART)

Ingredients: ¾ lb. (375 g.) minced or very finely chopped beef, 1–2 small ripe apples, 1 onion, fat, ¼–½ pt. (¼ l.) beef stock, salt, curry powder.

Peel and chop the onion and apples finely and sauté in hot fat. Add the meat and let it brown, stirring constantly, then add the stock. Add salt and curry powder, cover and simmer until done (about 15 minutes). Serve with fried potatoes, noodles or rice.

Chicken à la Mode
(GEFLÜGEL-AUFLAUF À LA MODE)

Ingredients: Meat of 1 cooked chicken, 2 apples, few cloves, 1–2 oz. (30–60 g.) butter, 1½–2 tbsp. breadcrumbs, pinch of sugar.

Peel, core and chop the apples. Chop the chicken. Put alternate layers of chicken and apple into a buttered heatproof dish with a few cloves to flavour. Melt the butter in a pan, add the sugar and breadcrumbs, then spread the mixture over the top. Bake in a moderate oven for 15–20 minutes.

Pineapple Chicken à la Hong Kong
HUHN MIT ANANAS À LA HONGKONG)

Ingredients: 1 roasting chicken, pepper, salt, fat, 1 large tin pineapple rings, juice of 1 lemon.

Joint the chicken and rub the pieces with salt and pepper. Heat the fat in a pan and brown the chicken pieces nicely all over. Add the syrup from the tin of pineapple, diluted with a little water. Cover the pan and cook until tender, basting frequently during cooking. Finally, flavour with lemon juice and adjust seasoning. Serve with a dish of boiled long-grained rice garnished with pineapple rings.

White wine may be used instead of pineapple syrup.

Turkish Chicken
(TÜRKISCHES HUHN)

Ingredients: 8 oz. (250 g.) white or black grapes, 2–3 glasses white wine, 1 roasting chicken, salt, olive oil, tinned pineapple juice.

Clean and wash the grapes and halve the larger ones. Place them in a bowl, cover with wine and leave for 1–2 hours. Meanwhile, joint and cook the chicken with the pineapple juice as above. Serve chicken on a dish garnished with the grapes.

Hamburg Duck
(HAMBURGER ENTENBRATEN MIT PFIFF)

Ingredients: 4 apples, cold roast duck, 1 onion, butter.

Chop the peeled apples, onion and the meat. Butter a heatproof dish, put a layer of apples on the bottom and a mixture of chopped duck and onion on top. Dot with butter and bake in a moderate oven for 20 minutes.

Breton Duck
(ENTE AUF BRETONISCHE ART)

Ingredients: 1 duck, salt, butter, 1 onion, 1 bay leaf, 1 glass brandy, pepper, salt, 2–3 apples, 3–4 slices lightly fried bread.

Place the prepared and trussed duck in a baking tin in which butter has been melted, and brown all over. Pour the brandy over the bird and set alight. Add the chopped onion, bay leaf and a little water, pepper and salt, and roast in a moderate oven for about 1 hour, basting frequently. Peel and core the apples and slice thinly. Cook briefly in a little butter and place on top of the fried bread. Carve the duck. Arrange the bread and apples on a serving dish, place the duck on top and serve.

Peaches may be used in the same way as the apples.

Duckling with Fruit à la Maison
(ENTE MIT OBST NACH ART DES HAUSES)

Ingredients: 1 duckling, salt, pepper, 3 cooking apples, handful of raisins, fat, flour, ½ glass port, morello cherries or sections of mandarin oranges.

Prepare the duck and wash. Rub the cavity with a little salt and pepper and stuff with the raisins and the apples which have been peeled, cored and chopped. Sew up the opening with needle and thread, brown all over in hot fat, add a little water and roast in a moderate oven until done. Baste frequently during cooking and turn once. Skim excess fat from the pan, add the port and thicken the gravy with flour if desired. Carve the bird and serve garnished with cherries or mandarin sections.

Prunes are used for the stuffing in Holstein.

Goose Stuffed with Fruit
(GANS MIT GEMISCHTER OBSTFÜLLE)

Ingredients: 1 goose (8–10 lb.), salt, fat, white wine, 2 sticks celery, 2 apples, 8 oz. (250 g.) grapes.

Prepare and wash the goose and rub with salt inside and out. Peel, core and chop the apples, cut the celery into thin strips and mix with the grapes. Stuff the bird with this mixture and sew up the opening. Brown in hot fat all over, pour wine and a little water over the bird and cook until tender. (Cooking times: 425°F, Mark 6 for 15 minutes, reduce to 350°F, Mark 3. Allow 25 minutes per pound for a stuffed bird.) Remove excess fat once or twice during cooking. Carve the goose and serve garnished with the stuffing. Hand the gravy round separately.

Goose Giblets
(GÄNSEKLEIN)

Ingredients: Giblets of goose (neck, wings, heart, stomach), bouquet garni, 1 onion, salt, 1 glass white wine, 4–5 oz. (125 g.) dried mixed fruit, 1 apple.

Wash the giblets and cook in water, together with the onion, bouquet garni, wine, dried fruit and salt until tender. Add the peeled, cored and quartered apples just before the end. Serve the giblets on a dish and arrange the fruit around them. A bechamel sauce can be poured over the fruit or handed round separately.

Game Hubertus
(WILDSCHLEGEL HUBERTUS)

Ingredients: Saddle of venison or wild boar (5–6 lb.) or 2 saddles of hare, vinegar, 2 onions, 1 bayleaf, peppercorns, 2 juniper berries, salt, fat, flour, 5 tsp. French mustard, 1 glass red wine, 1–2 oranges, sugar.

Make a marinade by mixing the vinegar with 1 chopped onion, the bayleaf, peppercorns, juniper berries and salt. Bring to the boil, leave to cool, and pour over the meat which has been placed in a deep bowl. Leave for 2 days, turning it occasionally. Lift out the meat and wipe it dry. Slice the second onion, brown in hot fat. Add the meat and brown all over. Pour the hot marinade over, cover and simmer gently until meat is tender (about 3 hours). Thicken the gravy with flour and add the wine and mustard. Carve the meat, arrange on a serving dish and garnish with sliced oranges. These are improved if simmered in a little water with sugar shortly before serving. Rings of pineapple and cherries steeped in brandy are an added improvement.

Turkish Fruit Pilaff

(TÜRKISCHER FRÜCHTEPILAFF)

Ingredients: 14 oz. (400 g.) rice, 1 onion, fat, salt, 3½–5 tsp. curry powder, 10½ oz. (300 g.) lamb or pork, 6 stewed prunes, 1 banana, 1 cooked peach, 3–4 pineapple rings, 5–8 tsp. mango chutney.

Cook the rice in fast boiling salted water for 12 minutes, drain and shake to separate the grains. Peel and finely chop the onion, mince or finely chop the meat. Heat the fat, fry onion and meat, add curry, cover and cook until tender. Slice the peach and banana. Mix the rice with the meat, arrange on a dish and garnish with the fruit and chutney.

Gammon à l'Americaine

(SCHINKENSTEAK À L'AMERICAINE)

Ingredients: 4 thick slices gammon or ham, 8 slices orange of the same thickness, 8 cloves, butter or margarine, cherry brandy.

Place 2 slices of orange on each steak together with 2 cloves and secure with cocktail sticks. Put slices into a shallow buttered heat-proof dish and bake in a moderate oven for 10–12 minutes. Remove the cloves, arrange on a serving dish and bring to the table. Pour the brandy over the steaks and set alight, or serve without flaming. They are delicious either way. Serve with a green salad.

Peking Stew

(PEKINGER STEW)

Ingredients: ¾–1 lb. (375–500 g.) pork or chicken, 2 large onions, fat, 3 juicy apples, ¾ pt. (½ l.) beef stock, salt, pepper, cinnamon, soya sauce.

Heat the fat, add the sliced onions and fry. Add the diced meat and cook for a short while. Transfer meat and onions to a buttered heatproof dish. Peel, core and slice the apples and distribute over the mixture. Season with salt, pepper and a pinch of cinnamon. Flavour the stock with soya sauce if desired, and pour over. Cook in a moderate oven. Serve with potato purée and green vegetables.

Aldermen's Special
(RATSHERRN-PLATTE)

Ingredients: 12–14 oz. (350–400 g.) pigs' kidneys, fat, flour, salt, 4 fl. oz. ($\frac{1}{10}$ l.) sour cream, 2–3 peaches, 1–2 mandarin oranges, butter.

Cut the kidneys in half and core, then slice thinly. Fry them quickly (3–4 minutes) in hot fat, lift out and keep warm. Make a roux from fat and flour, add the cream and season. Return the kidney to the sauce to heat, then arrange on a serving dish. Blanch the peaches to remove the skins and fry briefly in hot butter together with the mandarins. Garnish the kidney with the fruit and serve.

Rice Dish Teheran
(TEHERANER REISAUFLAUF)

Ingredients: 8 oz. (250 g.) rice, 1 lb. (500 g.) minced steak, 2 onions, fat, 1 small (2¼ oz. [70 g.]) tin tomato purée, paprika, curry powder, ¼ lb. (120 g.) mushrooms, butter, 5 pineapple rings, ½ banana, 5 compote cherries.

Wash and boil rice in the usual way, taking care to keep the grains whole, drain, spray with cold water, then keep hot. Chop the onions and fry until golden. Fry the meat and mix with the rice and tomato purée. Season well with paprika and curry powder. Melt some butter and gently cook the mushrooms in it. Butter a fairly deep heatproof dish and into it put alternating layers of rice mixture and mushrooms. Place the pineapple rings and sliced banana on top and bake in a moderate oven for 15–20 minutes. Garnish with cherries and serve with a green salad, with beer for the thirsty ones.

A satisfying and attractive dish.

Steak Ursula

Ingredients per person: 1 steak (beef, pork or veal), olive oil, salt, pepper, 1 pineapple ring, slices of orange or mandarin.

Flatten each steak and brush with oil. Fry or grill on both

sides according to thickness until done. Season with pepper and salt and serve on warmed plates. Garnish with the fruit.

Other possible garnishes are peach halves, previously blanched, poached in a little water and sprinkled with lemon juice or brandy; bananas brushed with butter and grilled; and cranberry compote.

French Fillet Steaks
(FRANZÖSISCHES FILET)

Ingredients: 4 fillet steaks (beef, pork or veal), salt, flour, fat, 1 lb. (500 g.) grapes.

Beat the fillets to flatten them. Sprinkle with salt, coat with flour and fry on both sides in hot fat. Arrange on a dish and garnish with grapes. Serve with French-fried potatoes.

Pork Fillet Steaks – Goerlitz Style
(GÖRLITZER GEWÜRZSCHNITZEL)

Ingredients: 4 pork fillet steaks, salt, 8 oz. (250 g.) prunes, fat, cinnamon, ground cloves, juice of 1 lemon, slices of lemon and mandarin orange.

Soak the prunes and remove the stones. Make an incision in each fillet with a sharp knife and widen it into a pocket. Stuff with prunes and sew up. Fry the fillets in hot fat until golden brown, add the remaining prunes and a little water, cover and cook until tender. Care should be taken that there is always sufficient liquid in the pan. Finally, add seasonings. Serve fillets in the gravy, garnished with slices of lemon and mandarin oranges.

Gourmet Schnitzel
(FEINSCHMECKER-SCHNITZEL)

Ingredients: 4 veal or pork fillet steaks, salt, 1 beaten egg, breadcrumbs, fat, 1–2 oranges, few stoned morello or other cherries, brandy.

Flatten the fillets, salt them and coat with egg and breadcrumbs. Fry gently in fat on both sides and arrange with a garnish of peeled, thinly sliced oranges and a few cherries which have been steeped in brandy.

Stuffed Schnitzel Ulrike
(GEFÜLLTES KALBSSCHNITZEL ULRIKE)

Ingredients: 4 veal escalopes, salt, fat, 2 bananas, juice of 1 lemon, 2½ tsp. condensed milk, 2 oz. (50 g.) ham or lean bacon.

Salt the fillets and fry in hot fat on both sides. It should take about 10–20 minutes, according to thickness. Meanwhile peel the bananas, pulp with a fork, add condensed milk and lemon juice and mix with the finely chopped ham. Divide the mixture into four and spread one portion on each of the cooked fillets. Roll up and secure with a cocktail stick. Serve hot.

Pork Chops à la Lorraine
(SCHWEINESTEAK AUF LOTHRINGER ART)

Ingredients: 4 pork chops, 4 apples, French mustard, breadcrumbs, fat, brandy.

Wash and dry the chops. Spread each with a little mustard and coat with breadcrumbs. Fry in fat on both sides until done, about 10 minutes according to thickness. Bake the apples in the oven or in a pan for about 8 minutes. After a few minutes sprinkle a little brandy on them and again before serving hot on a dish with the chops.

Instead of apples, rings of pineapple may be used in exactly the same way.

Westphalian Hot Pot
(WESTFÄLISCHES DURCHEINANDER)

Ingredients: ½ lb. (250 g.) white haricot beans, ½ lb. (250 g.) runner beans, 3–4 carrots, 5–6 large potatoes, 2 apples, 2 pears, 7 oz. (200 g.) bacon, salt, pepper, fat.

Chop the bacon, fry briefly and add the white beans, which should have been soaked in water overnight, together with their liquid. Prepare the runner beans, cut in half and add to the pan together with the peeled and sliced potatoes and carrots. Season and cook until tender, adding a little water if necessary. Just before the end add the peeled and diced fruit and cook for a few more minutes.

This is a very popular regional dish.

FISH WITH FRUIT

Hamburg Eel Soup
(HAMBURGER AAL-SUPPE)

Ingredients: 1 lb. (500 g.) eels, salt, nutmeg, 1 small tin garden peas, butter, breadcrumbs, fat, sage, 10–16 oz. (300–500 g.) mixed dried fruit, (plums, apricots, pears, apples), flour, vinegar, meat stock or white wine.

Skin the eels, cut into even pieces, season with salt and nutmeg, brush with melted butter and coat with breadcrumbs. Heat fat in a pan, add a little sage and fry the pieces of fish all over. Add stock or white wine to cover and cook until the fish is done. Lift the eel out of the liquid and cook the dried fruit until tender. Add the tinned peas, thicken the soup with flour and flavour with a dash of vinegar. Serve soup and fish separately.

Fresh fruit with a few prunes added can be used in place of dried fruit.

Herring Erikson
(HERINGSFILET ERIKSON)

Ingredients: 6–8 herring fillets, ¾–1 pt. (½ l.) sour cream, lemon juice or vinegar, 1–2 apples, 2 onions.

Place the fillets into a dish. Mix lemon juice or vinegar with the sour cream and pour over the fish. Peel and core the apples, slice thinly, slice the onions and scatter over the fillets. Leave for 1 hour then serve with boiled potatoes or rye bread.

Fish Fillets with Bananas
(FISCHFILET MIT BANANEN)

Ingredients: 5–6 oz. (150 g.) fillet per person, salt, pepper, breadcrumbs, condensed milk, fat, 2 bananas, lemon juice or butter.

Wash the fillets, season with salt and pepper, brush with milk and coat with breadcrumbs. Fry in hot fat on both sides. Slice the bananas and fry quickly in a separate pan. Garnish the fish with the fried bananas on a serving dish. Finally, sprinkle with lemon juice or browned butter.

Russian Carp
(KARPFEN AUF RUSSISCHE ART)

Ingredients: 1 carp, salt, 1¼ pt. (¾ l.) white wine, 1 knob butter, 3½–5 tbsp. flour, 2 onions, sauerkraut cooked in white wine with apples, sweet-and-sour plums, grated horseradish, condensed milk.

Clean the carp, remove the scales, wash and dry. Dust the fish with flour, place into a casserole with the butter and pour the wine over. Cook the fish until tender. Place it on a serving dish surrounded by the sauerkraut and garnish with fried onion rings. Serve with sweet-and-sour plums and horseradish mixed with condensed milk.

Fillet of Fish Cairo
(FISCHFILET 'KAIRO')

Ingredients: 5–6 oz. (150 g.) filleted fish (cod, haddock, etc., per person, salt, 1 egg, breadcrumbs, 2 onions) 2 cooking apples, fat, paprika, ¼–½ pt. (¼ l.) white wine, ½ pt. (¼ l.) meat stock, 1 tsp. potato flour.

Wash the fillets and sprinkle with salt. Coat them with beaten egg and breadcrumbs and fry in fat on both sides. Remove from the pan and keep warm. For the sauce, peel and slice the apples and onions and fry to a golden colour. Sprinkle with paprika and pour on the wine and stock. Thicken with potato flour and serve with the fish.

Fried Sole Istanbul
(PANIERTE ISTAMBULER SEEZUNGE)

Ingredients: 13 oz. (375 g.) sole fillets, olive oil or butter, breadcrumbs, pineapple rings or slices of orange.

Brush the fillets with oil or melted butter. Coat with breadcrumbs and fry in oil or butter until crisp. Serve with a garnish of pineapple or orange.

VEGETABLES WITH FRUIT

Sauerkraut with Apples Geneva
(GENFER ÄPFELKRAUT-SCHÜSSEL AUF FEINSCHMECKERART)

Ingredients: 1 lb. (500 g.) sauerkraut, 1 lb. (500 g.) ham or bacon, 3 large apples, beef stock, ½ pt. (⅓ l.) sour cream, fat.

Dice the bacon or ham, fry quickly and mix with the raw sauerkraut. Peel and core the apples and slice thinly. Put alternate layers of apples and sauerkraut into a buttered heat-proof dish, pour over the stock and finally the cream. Bake in a moderate oven for 1–1½ hours until the sauerkraut is done. A dash of champagne added just before the end of cooking time greatly improves the dish.

Sauerkraut Dolores
(SAUERKRAUT-SCHÜSSEL DOLORES)

Ingredients: 1 lb. (500 g.) sauerkraut, 1 onion, lard, 3 juniper berries, little apple juice or stock, 4 fl. oz. ($\frac{1}{16}$ l.) sour cream, 1 raw potato, 2 tbsp. pineapple juice, 1–2 pineapple rings.

Chop the onion, brown lightly in lard, add sauerkraut and juniper berries, pour over the fruit juice or stock and cook until done. Stir in the sour cream, thicken with the peeled and grated raw potato and flavour with the pineapple juice. Serve on a dish garnished with pineapple rings.

Cranberry compote or peach halves which have been lightly poached in a little sugar-syrup (3 ounce [90 gramme] sugar to ½ pint [¼ litre] water) are alternative garnishes. Pineapple juice can be used instead of apple juice.

An ideal accompaniment to roast poultry, game or pork.

Red Cabbage Maryland
(ROTKRAUT MARYLAND)

Ingredients: 1 small red cabbage, lard, salt, 2½–5 tsp. vinegar, 1–2 pears (not too sweet), 1 small apple, pine-apple pieces, sugar, 1 glass red wine.

Wash, quarter and shred the cabbage, removing the core. Cook in lard, covered, for a few minutes, adding salt and vinegar. Add water if necessary, but only the minimum amount required to prevent the contents burning. (The gourmet's cabbage should show no liquid.) Peel, core and slice the apple and pears thinly and add to the cabbage. Scatter pineapple pieces on top, pour over the wine and sprinkle with sugar.

For added improvement, stir in 5 teaspoons redcurrant jelly, or the same amount of cranberry jelly. In this case omit the pears and pineapple.

Red Cabbage Ticinio
(ROTKRAUT AUF TESSINER ART)

Ingredients: 1 small red cabbage, lard, 1–2 apples, 1 glass red wine, 8 oz. (250 g.) peeled and cooked chestnuts, 1½–3 oz. (50–100 g.) green bacon, salt, pepper, pinch of sugar, brandy.

Quarter the cabbage, remove central core and shred. Peel, core and dice the apples. Melt the lard, add the cabbage, apples, wine and seasonings, cover and simmer until tender. When the cabbage is almost cooked, dice the bacon, fry it in a pan and heat the chopped chestnuts with the bacon. Stir this mixture into the cabbage and add a dash of brandy just before serving.

Asparagus à la Madame
(SPARGEL À LA MADAME)

Ingredients: 2 lb. (1 kg.) asparagus, ¼ tsp. sugar, juice of 1–2 oranges, 2 egg yolks, 5½ oz. (150 g.) butter, pinch of paprika, nutmeg, slices of orange or mandarin.

Tie the asparagus into a bundle and steam until tender in water to which a little sugar has been added. In the meantime cook the orange juice over a low flame until it thickens. Cool. Melt the butter, leave to cool a little, stir in the orange juice and finally the yolks. Beat the sauce until creamy, season with paprika and nutmeg and pour over the cooked asparagus. Garnish with slices of orange or mandarin.

Baked Celeriac with Apples
(GEBACKENE SELLERIESCHEIBEN MIT ÄPFELN)

Ingredients: 3 medium-sized celeriac roots, salt, juice of 1 lemon, 1½ lb. (750 g.) apples, 1 lb. (500 g.) cooked potatoes, fat, flour, 1–2 egg yolks, breadcrumbs.

Peel the celeriac and cook in a little water containing salt and lemon juice until tender but still firm. Cut into slices about ½ inch thick and coat with flour, beaten yolk and breadcrumbs. Peel, slice and fry the potatoes and apples in a generous amount of fat. Fry the celeriac in a separate pan until crisp. Arrange the apples and potatoes in the centre of a serving dish and surround with celeriac.

White Beans with Apples
(WEISSES BOHNENGEMÜSE MIT ÄPFELN)

Ingredients: 10½ oz. (300 g.) white haricot beans, salt, 1 onion, fat, 13 oz. (375 g.) apples, 5 tbsp. sugar, flour.

Soak the beans overnight in plenty of water. Cook in salted water until tender (about 1–1½ hours). Chop the onion, heat fat and cook gently until transparent, add flour and make a roux. Strain the beans, add the liquid to the pan and then the beans. While the beans are cooking, peel, core and chop the apples and cook in a very little water with the sugar until soft. Serve the beans in a deep bowl and top with the apple purée.

Holstein Hot Pot with Pears
(HOLSTEINER BOHNENTOPF MIT BIRNEN)

Ingredients: ¾ lb. (375 g.) stewing beef, 1 onion, bouquet garni, 1 carrot, 1 lb. (500 g.) runner or tinned beans, 2–3 juicy pears, fat, flour, salt.

Place the beef in a pan together with the bouquet garni, onion and carrot. Bring to the boil in salted water and simmer until the meat is half done. Slice the beans, add to the pan and continue cooking until everything is tender. Peel, halve and core the pears. Remove bouquet garni and onion and add the pears. Make a roux from fat and flour and thicken the stock.

Braunschweig Cabbage
(BRAUNSHWEIGER GRÜNKOHLSCHÜSSEL)

Ingredients: 2–2¼ lb. (1 kg.) cabbage, 1–2 onions, 2–3 oz. (60–
90 g.) lard, 10½ oz. (300 g.) bacon, 10½ oz. (300 g.)
Mettwurst or boiling sausage, 3–4 pears, little
stock, salt, pepper.

Strip the cabbage leaves, remove the thick veins and blanch
in hot salted water. Chop very finely or put through the mincer.
Peel and chop the onions, heat the lard and cook the onions in
it. Add the cabbage, chopped bacon and sausage, the peeled,
cored and chopped pears, and stock. Season and cook until
tender. Serve with little potatoes.

Peasant Hot Pot with Pears
(BÄUERLICHE BIRNENSPEISE)

Ingredients: 1½ lb. (500–750 g.) pears, sugar, 2¼ lb. (1 kg.)
potatoes, 2 eggs, salt, nutmeg, 1½ oz. (30–50 g.)
butter, 1 onion, 2 oz. (50 g.) bacon, fat.

Peel, core and cut the pears into small pieces. Cook in water
with a little sugar, then place in a heatproof dish with a little
of the syrup. Peel and grate the potatoes, place in a napkin
or muslin bag and squeeze out surplus water. Beat the eggs,
add to the potatoes and season with salt and nutmeg. Put this
mixture on top of the pears. Melt the butter, pour over, and
bake in a moderate oven for 1–1¼ hours. Serve with a garnish
of fried onion rings and chopped bacon.

Apple-Potato Hot Pot
(APFEL-KARTOFFELEINTOPE)

Ingredients: 4½ lb. (2 kg.) potatoes, salt, butter, 7 oz. (200 g.)
bacon, fat, 1½ apples, sugar, white wine.

Peel and dice the potatoes and boil in salted water until tender.
Pour off some of the liquid and beat the potatoes to a stiff
purée. Add melted butter and the diced and fried bacon.
Arrange the purée on a dish and surround with slices of apple
which have been poached in a little white wine and sugar.

Desserts

PUDDINGS AND SWEET DISHES WITH FRUIT

Rice Cakes with Rhubarb
(REISBOULETTEN MIT RHABARBERKOMPOTT)

Ingredients: 10½ oz. (300 g.) rice, milk, salt, sugar, 2 eggs,
1 egg yolk, breadcrumbs, fat, cinnamon.

For the compote: 1 lb. (500 g.) rhubarb, 5 oz. (150 g.) sugar,
1 glass apple juice, 1 tbsp. potato flour, 1 pkt.
(1½ tbsp.) vanilla sugar, 1 banana.

Wash the rice, bring to the boil in water and drain. Cook until
tender in milk to which a pinch of salt and a little sugar have
been added. All the liquid should be absorbed. Beat the 2 eggs,
stir in and leave to cool. Form small round cakes, coat in
beaten yolk and breadcrumbs and fry in hot fat until crisp.
Serve sprinkled with a mixture of sugar and cinnamon.

For the compote, prepare the rhubarb, cut it into small
pieces and cook in apple juice and sugar. Thicken with potato
flour, flavour with vanilla sugar and puréed banana.

Bread Pudding with Cherries

(KIRSCHEN-WECKPUDDING)

Ingredients: 6 rolls, ½ pt. (¼–⅜ l.) milk, 4½ oz. (125 g.) margarine, 3½ oz. (100 g.) sugar, 4 eggs, grated rind of 1 lemon, pinch of cinnamon, 1 lb. (500 g.) cherries, butter, breadcrumbs.

Cut the rolls into small pieces, soak in warm milk and squeeze out surplus liquid. Cream the margarine with the sugar and egg yolks, add flavourings, then fold in the stiffly beaten egg whites and stoned cherries. Add the crumbled bread mixture. Butter a pudding basin, sprinkle with breadcrumbs, fill with the mixture and steam for 45 minutes. Serve with fruit juice, chocolate sauce or wine sauce.

English Cherry Pie

(ENGLISCHE KIRSCHENPASTETE)

Ingredients: 7 oz. (200 g.) flour, 3½ oz. (100 g.) margarine, 1 egg, grated rind of ½ lemon, 9½ oz. (265 g.) sugar, breadcrumbs, 1¾ oz. (50 g.) butter, 1 oz. (30 g.) shredded almonds.

For the filling: 1 lb. (500 g.) black cherries, 1½ oz. (50 g.) sugar, 3 sweet rusks, 1 glass brandy.

Prepare the pastry by working together the flour, margarine, lemon rind, egg and 7 ounces (200 grammes) sugar. Chill for 1 hour, roll out, line a flan ring with threequarters of the pastry and sprinkle generously with breadcrumbs. Wash and stone the cherries, mix with the sugar and grated rusks and add the brandy. Fill the pastry case. Roll out the remaining pastry and place on top. Melt the butter, stir in 2½ ounces (65 grammes) sugar and the almonds, and brush over the pie. Bake in a moderate oven for 30 minutes (375°F, Mark 5).

Clafoutis [French Cherry Pudding]

(FRANZÖSISCHES KIRSCHENSPEISE)

Ingredients: 1½ lb. (500–750 g.) black cherries, dash of brandy, grated rind of ½ lemon, 3 eggs, 3½ oz. (100 g.) sugar, 1 tsp. cinnamon, 3 oz. (80–100 g.) flour, 2 small tins condensed milk, milk, butter, extra sugar and cinnamon.

Wash and stone the cherries. Butter a deep heatproof dish, put the cherries in and pour the brandy over. Beat the eggs with sugar and grated lemon rind, stir in cinnamon, flour, condensed milk and enough milk to give the mixture the consistency of a thick pancake batter. Pour this over the cherries and bake in a preheated oven for about 30 minutes at moderate heat. Test by inserting a metal skewer or fork. When it comes out without any batter clinging to it, the pudding is done. Dust with sugar and cinnamon and serve hot.

Plums can be used in the same way.

Pancake Pudding with Cherries
(PALATSCHINKENPUDDING MIT KIRSCHEN)

Ingredients: 10½ oz. (300 g.) cherries, jam, fat, butter, breadcrumbs, 2 tbsp. potato flour, ½ pt. (¼ l.) milk, 3½ tbsp. sugar, juice and grated rind of ½ lemon, 3 eggs, salt, cherry liqueur.
For the pancakes: 2¼ oz. (65 g.) flour, 1–2 eggs, ¼ pt. (⅛ l.) milk, pinch of salt.

Prepare a pancake batter. Fry thin pancakes, spread each with a little jam, then scatter stoned cherries on top and roll up. Leave to cool and cut in half. Butter a pudding dish, sprinkle with breadcrumbs and arrange the pancake rolls in it. Stir the potato flour into the milk, add the sugar, lemon juice and grated rind, the beaten eggs and salt. Pour the mixture over the pancakes, cover and steam for 40–50 minutes. Turn out and serve sprinkled with cherry liqueur.

Cherry Peter
(KIRSCHENPETER)

Ingredients: 2 lb. (1 kg.) cherries, 6–8 stale rolls, ¼–½ pt. (¼ l.) milk, 3–4 eggs, 2–3½ oz. (60–100 g.) sugar, 2 oz. (60 g.) butter or margarine, ¾ tsp. cinnamon, grated rind of 1 lemon, chopped almonds.

Wash and stone the cherries. Slice the rolls, steep in milk, lift out and crumble or put through the mincer. Cream sugar, butter or margarine and egg yolks thoroughly, add the flavourings, bread mixture and the cherries. Finally, fold in the stiffly beaten egg whites, place in a greased basin and bake for 50–60 minutes in a moderate oven. Serve hot with vanilla custard or cold as a cake. Sprinkle with chopped almonds if desired.

Use plums as an alternative fruit.

Viennese Raspberry Pudding
(WIENER HIMBEERAUFLAUF MIT BRANDTEIG)

Ingredients: 8 fl. oz. ($\frac{1}{4}$ l.) milk, 1 oz. (30 g.) butter, 4$\frac{1}{2}$ oz. (125 g.) flour, pinch of baking powder, 3 eggs, grated rind of $\frac{1}{2}$ lemon, 1 lb. (500 g.) raspberries, 1 pkt. (1$\frac{1}{2}$ tbsp.) vanilla sugar, butter, sugar, icing sugar.

Put the milk and butter into a saucepan and bring to the boil. Take it off the stove when the butter has melted and add all the flour, to which the baking powder has already been added. Stir vigorously until the paste is quite smooth and leaves the sides of the pan. Set aside to cool. Whisk the eggs lightly and add to the mixture one by one. The finished paste should be quite smooth. Add the grated lemon rind. Fill the bottom of a buttered heatproof dish with half the mixture, cover with raspberries, sprinkle with sugar and vanilla sugar and top with the remainder of the paste. Bake in a moderate oven for 40 minutes. To ensure good results do not open the oven for the first 30 minutes. Dust with icing sugar and serve hot.

Fried Elderflower Cakes from Grandmother's Cookbook
(HOLDER-[HOLUNDER-]KÜCHEL AUS GROSSMUTTERS KOCHBUCH)
Make a thin batter from 1$\frac{3}{4}$ pints (1 litre) milk, $\frac{1}{2}$ pound (250 grammes) flour, 3 eggs and melted butter. Dip heads of blossoming elderflowers into the mixture and fry quickly in hot fat.

Apricot Dumplings
(APRIKOSENKNÖDEL)

Ingredients: 1 lb. (500 g.) boiled potatoes, 8 oz. (250 g.) flour, 2 oz. (60 g.) margarine or butter, 1–2 eggs, pinch of salt, 1 lb. (500 g.) apricots, sugar cubes, breadcrumbs, butter.

Put the potatoes through a potato press or mincer. Turn on to a floured board, add flour, margarine, eggs and salt and knead all the ingredients together until smooth. Shape into a thick roll, then cut off rounds about 1 inch thick. Flatten each piece by hand and wrap around an apricot in which the stone has been replaced by a sugar cube. Care must be taken to pinch the edges well together. Bring a pan of salted water to the boil, drop the dumplings in and leave to simmer for 15 minutes. Lift the dumplings out, place on a serving dish and sprinkle with breadcrumbs fried in butter. The flavour of these dumplings is improved if the apricots are first blanched and skinned.

Instead of apricots, the dumplings may be filled with plums, cherries (3 in each dumpling, unstoned), greengages or pear slices.

This is a national dish in Austria and is often served with vanilla custard.

Livanzen
(LIWANZEN)

Ingredients: 13 oz. (375 g.) flour, 2 eggs, ¾ oz. (20 g.) sugar, knob of butter or margarine, pinch of salt, ¾ oz. (20 g.) yeast, ⅝ pt. (⅜ l.) milk, fat, fresh soft fruit or compote, little sugar.

Make a thin batter from all the ingredients, except fat, fruit and a little sugar, beating well. Leave for 1 hour. Heat fat in a pan and drop quantities of the batter into the fat as for pancakes. Fry on both sides. The cakes will rise during cooking. Serve on a warm plate topped with spoonfuls of fruit and sprinkled with sugar.

Fruit Rissoles
(OBST-POLPETTEN)

Ingredients: 1 lb. (500 g.) cherry plums, 7 oz. (200 g.) oatmeal, 3 oz. (80 g.) butter or margarine, ¾ tsp. cinnamon, 3½ oz. (100 g.) flour, 1–2 eggs, fat, sugar.

Wash and stone the plums and cook them in very little water until quite soft. Fry the oatmeal in butter until golden. Separate the egg(s). Mix the oatmeal with the fruit pulp and stir in the flour, egg yolk(s) and cinnamon. Fold in the stiffly beaten egg white(s). With floury hands, form little cakes from the mixture and fry in hot fat until crisp. Dust with sugar and serve with vanilla custard or fruit syrup.

Swiss Plum Pudding
(SCHWEIZER ZWETSCHGENSCHOBER)

Ingredients: 1¾ lb. (750 g.) stoned plums, 3–3½ oz. (80–100 g.) butter, 3 oz. (80 g.) sugar, 3 eggs, grated rind of ½ lemon, 7 oz. (200 g.) semolina, ½ pt. (¼ l.) sour cream or sour milk, ½ pt. (¼ l.) milk, breadcrumbs, extra sugar, cinnamon.

Butter a heatproof dish and sprinkle with breadcrumbs. Arrange the plums in it. Combine all the other ingredients, except the egg whites, cinnamon and extra sugar, and beat well. Beat the whites stiffly and fold into the mixture. Spread over the fruit and bake in a moderate oven for 50–60 minutes. Sprinkle a mixture of sugar and cinnamon on top and serve hot.

Plum Dumpling Pudding
(ÜBERBACKENE ZWETSCHGENNUDELN)

Ingredients: 1 lb. (500 g.) boiled potatoes, ½ lb. (250 g.) flour, 2½ oz. (60–80 g.) butter or margarine, 1 egg, pinch of salt, 1½ lb. (750 g.) stoned plums, same number of blanched almonds as plums, 2 oz. (60 g.) butter, breadcrumbs, sugar.

Put the potatoes through a potato press or mincer. Work well together with the flour, butter or margarine, egg and salt into a smooth dough. Put an almond and a little sugar into each plum. Roll out the dough on a board, cut into strips 2 inches wide and cut rectangles from the strips. Wrap each plum in a rectangle, leaving one end open. Grease a heatproof dish with plenty of butter and arrange the plum dumplings in it. Any left-over plums can be placed evenly between the dumplings to make a chessboard effect. Bake in a moderate oven. Fry the breadcrumbs in butter, sprinkle over the top and serve with vanilla custard, sugar or plum compote.

Instead of plums, cherries, greengages or cherry plums may be used. Curd cheese can replace the potatoes in the dumpling mixture, in which case there should be equal quantities of curd cheese, flour and butter or margarine.

Stuffed Plums
(GEFÜLLTE ZWETSCHGENSPALTEN)

Ingredients: 10½ oz. (300 g.) flour, 1–2 eggs, pinch of salt, 1¾ tsp. grated lemon rind, 1 pt. (½ l.) milk, 1½ lb. (500–750 g.) plums, same number of blanched almond as plums, 3½ oz. (100 g.) dessicated coconut, fat, icing sugar, cinnamon.

Combine flour, eggs, salt, grated lemon rind and enough milk to make a thick coating batter. Beat well. Remove the stones from the plums and replace each with an almond and a little coconut. Dip each plum in the batter and fry in deep fat. While still hot, dip the plums in a mixture of icing sugar and cinnamon and arrange on a dish.

Stuffed Plums, Morello Cherries or Cherries from Grandmother's Cookbook
(GEBACKENE ZWETSCHGEN, WEICHSEL ODER KIRSCHEN AUS GROSSMUTTERS KOCHBUCH)

Prepare a choux pastry as for Viennese Raspberry Pudding. Stone the plums and replace stones with blanched almonds. Coat each plum with choux pastry and fry in hot fat. Sprinkle with sugar and serve hot. Cherries are treated in the same way except that only half the stem is cut off, the rest being left on for easy handling.

Rice Pudding with Apples
(GEBACKENER ÄPFELREIS)

Ingredients: ½ lb. (250 g.) rice, ¾ pt. (½ l.) milk or wine, lemon rind, pinch of salt, 5 oz. (150 g.) sugar, 1½ lb. (750 g.) apples, 1½ oz. (50 g.) sultanas, small glass rum, 2 egg whites, 1 pkt. (1½ tbsp.) vanilla sugar, butter.

Wash the rice and boil in water for 5–7 minutes. Drain, add the wine or milk, lemon rind, salt and about 1½ ounces (50 grammes) sugar and continue to cook until tender. Meanwhile peel, core and slice the apples. Stew them in a very little water for a short time, with a pat of butter, 1½ ounces (50 grammes) sugar and the sultanas. The apple slices should be still firm and there should not be too much liquid. Into a greased heat-proof dish put alternate layers of rice and apples and pour the rum over the topmost layer of fruit. The top layer should be rice. Bake in a moderate oven for 10–15 minutes. Beat the egg whites stiffly, fold in the remaining sugar and the vanilla sugar, fill a forcing bag with the mixture and pipe a lattice across the top. Return to the oven for 5 minutes.

Yeast Pancakes with Apples
(HEFEPLINSEN MIT ÄPFELN)

Ingredients: ½ lb. (200 g.) flour, ¼ oz. (10 g.) yeast, 1¾ tsp. sugar, pinch of salt, grated rind of ½ lemon, ½ pt. (¼ l.) milk, 1 lb. (500 g.) apples, fat, extra sugar.

Cream the yeast with the sugar and 1–2 tablespoons milk, leave in a warm place for 10 minutes. Add the flour, salt, grated lemon rind and the remainder of the milk. Knead well until the dough is soft and elastic. Cover with a cloth and leave in a warm place for ½–¾ hour. Meanwhile peel, core and slice the apples. Add apple slices to the dough, heat fat in a pan and fry pancakes until golden on both sides. Serve hot. The pancakes may be dusted with sugar before serving.

Alternatively, fry the cakes plain and scatter the fruit slices on top. Pears may be used instead of apples.

Apple Bits
(APFELMUNDBISSEN)

Ingredients: 18 oz. (500 g.) flour, 3½ oz. (100 g.) butter or margarine, 2 oz. (60 g.) sugar, pinch of salt, grated rind of 1 lemon, ¾ oz. (20 g.) yeast, ¼ pt. (⅛ l.) milk, 1 lb. (500 g.) apples, egg yolk, extra sugar.

Cream the yeast with 1 teaspoon sugar and a little lukewarm milk. Make into a dough using all the remaining ingredients, except the apples, egg yolk and extra sugar. Knead until smooth and leave in a warm place to rise. It may be necessary to add a little more milk. When risen, roll out the dough thinly, cut out rounds about 3 inches in diameter. Peel, core and dice the apples, put a few pieces on each round of dough, brush the edges of the dough with beaten egg and fold together. Put on to a greased warmed baking tin, leave to rise once more, brush with egg and bake in a moderate oven for 20–30 minutes. Arrange the bits on a dish and dust with sugar. Serve with hot chocolate sauce or vanilla custard if desired.

Apple Slices from Grandmother's Cookbook
(APFELSCHNITTEN AUS GROSSMUTTERS KOCHBUCH)
Peel, core and slice some apples, pour wine over them and leave for 1–2 hours. Coat with flour, fry in hot fat, sprinkle with sugar and serve.

Hapsburg Apple Pudding
(HABSBURGER APFELAUFLAUF)
Ingredients: 2¼ lb. (1 kg.) juicy apples, 3 oz. (80 g.) butter or margarine, 5½ oz. (150 g.) sugar, 6 oz. (170 g.) jam, 1 oz. (30 g.) shredded almonds or hazelnuts, juice of 1½ lemons, slices of bread.

Peel, core and slice the apples and cook gently in a little of the butter with the sugar, adding water if necessary. The apples should remain firm. Line a heatproof dish with thin slices of bread, sprinkle with melted butter and spread with diluted jam. Fill the dish with apple slices, sprinkle with shredded almonds or hazelnuts and flavour with lemon juice. Top with a layer of bread. Dot with butter and bake in a moderate oven for 20–30 minutes. Serve hot with vanilla custard.

Peaches or apricots may be used instead of apples.

Stockholm Apples
(STOCKHOLMER APFELSPEISE)
Ingredients: Purée of 3¼ lb. (1½ kg.) apples, grated rind of ½ orange, 2½–5 tsp. rum, 2 oz. (50 g.) butter, 2 oz. (50 g.) sugar, 2½ oz. (70 g.) flour, pinch of cinnamon.

Flavour the purée with grated orange rind and rum, then pile into a buttered mould. Combine sugar, flour and cinnamon add the melted butter, crumble the mixture with your fingers and distribute on top of the purée. Bake in a moderate oven for 10 minutes.

A layer of finely chopped almonds may be put between the fruit and the sugar mixture for added interest.

Apples on Parade
(ÄPFEL-PARADE)

Ingredients: 4–6 juicy apples, flour, 1 egg, breadcrumbs, fat, jam or chopped almonds.

At the stalk end cut a slice off each apple. Peel and carefully remove the cores. Roll the apples in flour, brush with beaten egg and coat with breadcrumbs. Fry in hot fat, remove and stuff with jam or almonds. Replace the lids, arrange the fruit on a dish and serve with a sweet sauce.

Apple Charlotte
(APFEL-CHARLOTTE)

Ingredients: 1½ lb. (750 g.) apples, 8 oz. (250 g.) sugar, juice of 1 lemon, butter, biscuits, cake or slices of bread, fruit juice or white wine.

Peel the apples, slice and remove the cores. Put the sugar in a pan with about 1¾ pints (1 litre) water and cook until the sugar has dissolved. Add the lemon juice and piece by piece the apple slices and simmer until they become transparent. Butter a heatproof pudding dish and line with a layer of biscuits. Lift out the apple slices, put a layer in the pudding dish and top with another layer of biscuits. Moisten with wine or fruit juice and continue in this way until the dish is filled. The top layer should be biscuits. Bake in a moderate oven for 50–60 minutes. Turn out (after leaving it to set for a few minutes) or serve in the dish. Accompany with a caramel sauce, cold milk or cream.

Anatolian Rice Dish
(ANATOLISCHE REISSPEISE)

Ingredients: 14–21 oz. (440–655 g.) rice, $\frac{3}{4}$–$1\frac{1}{4}$ pt. ($\frac{1}{2}$–$\frac{3}{4}$ l.) white wine, pieces of fresh lemon rind, $3\frac{1}{2}$ tbsp. sugar, 5 tbsp. mixed dried fruit, $3\frac{1}{2}$ tbsp. shredded almonds, 1 orange.

Wash the rice and bring to the boil. Drain, separate the grains with cold water then cook with the wine, pieces of lemon rind and a little sugar until tender but not mushy. Remove the lemon rind, add the remaining sugar, dried fruit and almonds and mix well together. If necessary, add a little wine and sweeten to taste. Arrange on a dish or on individual plates and garnish with orange slices. Serve yogurt with this nutritious and refreshing dish.

Poor Knights with Compote
(ARME RITTER MIT KOMPOTT)

Ingredients: 6–8 rolls, $\frac{1}{2}$ pt. ($\frac{1}{4}$–$\frac{3}{8}$ l.) milk, 9 oz. (250 g.) flour, 2 eggs, pinch of salt, fat, sugar, cinnamon, fruit compote.

Pour half the milk into a bowl, slice the rolls and soak in the milk. With the rest of the milk, flour, eggs and salt prepare a batter, dip the bread slices into it and fry in hot fat until golden brown on both sides. Sprinkle with sugar and cinnamon and serve hot with any fruit compote.

Tall John with Compote
(GROSSER HANS MIT KOMPOTT)

Ingredients: 10 stale rolls or bread, milk, $2\frac{1}{2}$ oz. (75 g.) butter or margarine, 2 eggs, $\frac{1}{2}$ pt. ($\frac{1}{4}$ l.) milk, $1\frac{1}{2}$ oz. (50 g.) raisins, $\frac{3}{4}$ tsp. cinnamon, pinch of salt, breadcrumbs, fruit compote.

Slice the rolls, or their equivalent in bread, soak in the milk, squeeze out the surplus moisture and mash or put through the mincer. Separate the eggs. Cream the butter with the yolks, add the raisins, milk, bread and finally, the stiffly beaten whites. Add salt and cinnamon. Grease a pudding basin, sprinkle with breadcrumbs and fill with the mixture. Cover tightly and steam for 1 hour. Uncover, leave for a few minutes, turn out on to a serving dish and serve with hot or cold compote.

Pineapple Carlton
(ANANAS-CARLTON)

Ingredients: 8 pineapple rings, 8 oz. (250 g.) pudding rice, 1 pt. ($\frac{1}{2}$ l.) white wine, 2 eggs, 1 glass Maraschino, $1\frac{1}{2}$ oz. (50 g.) sugar, 1 banana, 8 oz. (250 g.) grapes.

Coat the inside of a pudding basin with lightly caramelized sugar. Cook the rice with the wine and sugar for a few minutes. Sprinkle half the pineapple rings with sugar and dice the other half. Beat the eggs well, combine with rice and diced pineapple and add the liqueur. Pile into the pudding basin and steam for 1 hour. Turn out and decorate with pineapple rings, sliced banana and the grapes.

Pineapple Beignets
(ANANASBEIGNETS)

Ingredients: 1 large tin pineapple rings, fat.

For the batter: 8 oz. (200 g.) flour, 2 eggs, pinch of salt, grated rind of $\frac{1}{2}$ lemon, $\frac{1}{2}$ tsp. cooking oil, $\frac{1}{2}$ pt. ($\frac{1}{4}$ l.) milk.

Drain the pineapple rings. Prepare a batter from the egg yolks and the other ingredients. Stiffly beat the egg whites and fold in. Coat the pineapple rings with batter and fry in hot fat.

COMPOTES

Compote can be made from any fruit. It can be served cold as a pleasant sweet course, or hot as an accompaniment to a pudding or similar confection. In the sickroom, compote is always welcomed by the invalid, unless ruled out by the doctor for dietary reasons.

Preparation is quick and simple. Suitable flavourings

include lemon rind, lemon juice, cinnamon sticks, cloves and (adults only!) a dash of wine or liqueur. To keep the delicate flavour of the fruit intact, the fruit itself should never be allowed to boil for any length of time. It is better to prepare the syrup, let it boil up 2 or 3 times, pour it over the fruit and leave it to cool. This applies especially to soft fruit such as strawberries and raspberries, but also to peaches, apricots and grapes.

Rhubarb Compote
(RHABARBERKOMPOTT)

Ingredients: 1½ lb. (500–750 g.) rhubarb, rind of 1 lemon, 5–7 oz. (150–200 g.) sugar, 1 pkt. (1½ tbsp.) vanilla sugar.

Prepare the rhubarb and cut into small pieces. Gently cook with the lemon rind in ¼–½ pint (¼–½ litre) water for 4–5 minutes and sweeten with the sugar and vanilla sugar. Serve with biscuits or sponge fingers.

The acid taste which makes this fruit unpopular with some, people can be neutralized by the addition of ½–1 mashed banana.

Cherry Compote
(KIRSCHENKOMPOTT)

Ingredients: 1¾ lb. (750 g.) cherries, 3½ oz. (100 g.) sugar, 1 stick cinnamon, rind of ½ lemon, 1¾ tsp. potato flour.

Wash and stone the cherries. Add sugar, cinnamon, and lemon rind to 1¼ pints (¾ litre) water and bring to the boil. Add the cherries and simmer for 5–10 minutes. Thicken with the potato flour and chill. Remove cinnamon and lemon rind before serving.

By adding wine the compote may be served as a cold soup.

Strawberry Compote
(ERDBEERKOMPOTT)

Ingredients: 1 lb. (500 g.) strawberries, 4–5 oz. (125–150 g.) sugar, dash of alcohol (white wine, brandy or rum).

Boil the sugar with 1 pint (½ litre) water. When the syrup begins to thicken add the fruit. Bring to the boil and chill. Add wine or spirit before serving.

Grape Compote
(TRAUBENKOMPOTT)

Prepare in the same way as strawberry compote.

Redcurrant Compote
(JOHANNISBEERKOMPOTT)

Ingredients: 1½ lb. (500–750 g.) redcurrants, 5–7 oz. (150–200 g.) sugar.

Prepare and wash the fruit, add the sugar and ¼ pint (⅛ litre) water and cook until soft. Drain. If the syrup is too thin, continue to cook it separately. More sugar may be added to taste. Pour the syrup over the fruit and serve.

Gooseberry Compote
(STACHELBEERKOMPOTT)

Ingredients: 1½ lb. (500–750 g.) gooseberries, rind of ½ lemon, ½ vanilla pod, 5½ oz. (150 g.) sugar.

Put all the ingredients in a pan with 1 pint (½ litre) water, bring to the boil and simmer for a short time. The gooseberries should remain whole. Drain, remove vanilla pod and lemon rind and continue to simmer the syrup until it thickens. Pour over the fruit and serve.

Peach and Apricot Compote
(PFIRSICH- UND APRIKOSENKOMPOTT)

Ingredients: 1¾ lb. (750 g.) peaches or apricots, 5½ oz. (150 g.) sugar, 1 pkt. (1½ tbsp.) vanilla sugar.

Blanch the fruit, skin, halve and remove the stones. Cut into thick slices. Make the syrup by boiling together the sugar and 1 pint (½ litre) water and pour it over the fruit. If these are not quite ripe leave them to simmer for a short time in the syrup. Arrange in a dish and sprinkle with vanilla sugar. Chill and serve with or without cream.

Raspberry Compote

(HIMBEERKOMPOTT)

Ingredients: 1½ lb. (500–750 g.) raspberries, sugar, rind of ½ lemon, white wine.

Clean the raspberries and bring to the boil with sugar and lemon rind. Flavour with wine and chill.

To prepare a delicious cream, strain the fruit through a sieve, combine the resulting juice with 3–5 eggs and a little more sugar, then whisk the mixture in the top of a double saucepan until thick. Serve chilled.

Bilberry Compote

(HEIDELBEERKOMPOTT)

Ingredients: 1½ lb. (500–750 g.) bilberries, 3½–5½ oz. (100–150 g.) sugar.

Clean and wash the bilberries, drain and simmer with the sugar until juice has formed and the fruit is tender.

Cranberry Compote

(PREISELBEERKOMPOTT)

Ingredients: 1½ lb. (500–750 g.) cranberries, 10–16 oz. (300–450 g.) sugar, piece of lemon rind.

Prepare as above, adding a piece of lemon during the cooking.

Plum Compote

(ZWETSCHGENKOMPOTT)

Ingredients: 1½ lb. (750 g.) plums, 5 oz. (150 g.) sugar, 1 stick cinnamon, rind of ½ lemon, 2 glasses red wine.

Wash, stone and halve the plums. Bring the wine and an equal amount of water to the boil with the sugar, cinnamon and lemon rind. Simmer for a few minutes and add the plums. Cook until the syrup thickens but do not let the fruit disintegrate. Remove cinnamon and lemon rind before serving.

This compote goes well with semolina slices, flummeries and milk puddings, or serve it diluted with wine and garnished with meringue 'snowflakes' as a refreshing first course on a summer's day.

Simple Pear Compote
(EINFACHES BIRNENKOMPOTT)

Ingredients: 1–1¾ lb. (500–750 g.) ripe pears, 2 cloves, lemon rind, sugar, 1 glass red wine.

Peel the pears, core, slice and cook in the wine with the cloves, lemon rind, a little sugar and water. Remove cloves and lemon rind. The pears can now be rubbed through a sieve and the resulting purée should not be too thin. Strain the syrup off first and add enough of it afterwards to obtain the required consistency.

Serve with pancakes, yeast dumplings, puddings, cereals or mixed with cranberry compote as a dessert.

Fruit Trio
(OBST-TRIO)

Ingredients: 2–3 ripe pears, 1–2 apples, ¾–1¼ lb. (375–500 g.) plums, stick cinnamon, rind of ½ lemon, sugar.

Peel, core and slice the apples and pears. Parboil the pears in a little water with half the cinnamon. Put in the apples and lemon rind and cook a little longer. Wash and stone the plums, add to the other fruit with the remaining cinnamon and cook until tender. Take off the heat and add sugar, taking care to keep the fruits whole. Remove cinnamon and lemon rind and cool.

Serve with puddings and sponges.

Apple Compote
(APFELKOMPOTT)

Ingredients: 2–2¼ lb. (1 kg.) apples, lemon rind, ½ stick cinnamon, handful of raisins, 1 pkt. (1½ tbsp.) vanilla sugar, sugar.

Peel, core and quarter the apples and poach in a little water with the lemon rind, cinnamon and washed raisins. Leave to cool, remove lemon rind, cinnamon and washed raisins. Leave to cool, remove lemon rind and cinnamon and flavour with vanilla sugar and sugar to taste.

A dash of brandy improves the compote.

Apple Purée
(APFELMUS)

Ingredients: 2 lb. (1 kg.) apples, ½ pt. (¼ l.) white wine, 2½ oz.
(80 g.) sugar, 6 tbsp. grated brown bread, sugar,
cinnamon.

Core and quarter the apples and cook in a little water until
tender. Rub through a sieve, sweeten the purée and flavour
with wine. Arrange in a serving bowl and sprinkle a mixture
of grated bread, sugar and cinnamon on top.

As an improvement to the purée, fold in the stiffly beaten
whites of 1–2 eggs, pile the mixture into a pudding tin or dish,
sprinkle on the topping and bake the pudding in a hot oven
for 10–15 minutes.

Apple Compote from Grandmother's Cookbook
(APFELKOMPOTT AUS GROSSMUTTERS KOCHBUCH)

Peel and core some sweet ripe apples, place them in a pan,
add a little wine and water in equal proportions together with
sugar, cinnamon and a piece of lemon rind, and poach until
tender. Place them on a dish and stuff the openings with redcurrant or morello compote. Return the strained juice to the
pan with some more sugar, bring to the boil once more and
pour over the apples. The juice should not come more than
halfway up the fruit.

Banana Compote
(BANANENKOMPOTT)

Ingredients: 3–4 bananas, juice of 3 oranges and 1 lemon,
3½–5 tbsp. sugar, 1 pkt. (1½ tbsp.) vanilla sugar,
grated rind of ½ orange.

Put the sliced bananas into a pan with the fruit juice and sugar
and simmer for a short time. Serve on a dish sprinkled with
grated orange rind and vanilla sugar.

Banana Cinnamon Compote
(BANANEN-ZIMTSPEISE)

Ingredients: 1½–1¾ lb. (750 g.) bananas, juice of 2 oranges and
1 lemon, 1¾ oz. (50 g.) sugar, pinch of cinnamon,
½ glass red wine.

Slice the bananas, put into a pan, add the fruit juice and sugar and simmer for a few minutes. Remove from heat, flavour with wine, cinnamon and a little more sugar, and cool.

Serve with rice pudding or semolina slices.

Orange Compote
(UNGEKOCHTES ORANGENKOMPOTT)

Ingredients: 1½–1¾ lb. (750 g.) oranges, 5–5½ oz. (150 g.) sugar, ¼–½ pt. (¼ l.) white wine or water, 1 tbsp. brandy, 2–3 tbsp. ground almonds or hazelnuts.

Peel the oranges, remove the pith and slice. Cook sugar and wine or water until the syrup is clear. Pour over the orange slices and leave to cool. Sprinkle with nuts and add brandy if desired.

Other kinds of fruit may be treated in the same way.

Rosehip and Grape Compote from Grandmother's Cookbook
(HAGEBUTTEN- UND WEINBEERCOMPOTT AUS GROSSMUTTERS KOCHBUCH)

Cook equal quantities of rosehips and grapes with wine, water and sugar until tender, and serve sprinkled with pistachio nuts or chopped lemon rind.

Samba Compote
(SAMBA-KOMPOTT)

Ingredients: 1½ lb. (500–750 g.) rhubarb, rind of ½ lemon, 5¼ oz. (150 g.) sugar, 1 pkt. (1½ tbsp.) vanilla sugar, ¼ lb. (100 g.) each strawberries, redcurrants and cherries, 1 banana.

Prepare the rhubarb, cut into small pieces, simmer with sugar and lemon rind in ½–1 pint (¼–½ litre) water. Drain and add vanilla sugar. Prepare the soft fruits (stone the cherries) and mix with the rhubarb in a glass bowl.

Give extra flavour to the rhubarb with a dash of white wine if desired, and pour some over the compote, or serve separately.

Quince Compote

(QUITTENKOMPOTT)

Ingredients: 1–1¼ lb. (500 g.) quinces, 7 oz. (200 g.) sugar, 1 pkt.
(1½ tbsp.) vanilla sugar.

Brush the quinces well, peel, core and quarter. Place them in a
pan, cover with water and cook for 1 hour. Flavour with sugar
and vanilla sugar. Should there be too much syrup, reduce it
by boiling separately a little longer. Serve chilled.

Rosehip Compote

(HAGEBUTTENKOMPOTT)

Ingredients: 1½ lb. (750 g.) ripe rosehips, 4 oz. (125 g.) sugar,
juice of ½ lemon, 1 stick cinnamon.

Quarter the rosehips, remove stems and pips, wash well and
cook with the other ingredients in a scant ½ pint (¼ litre)
water until tender. Rub through a sieve. Should the resulting
purée be too thick, add a little more water. Serve at once.

Rosehips are particularly rich in vitamins and their relative
neglect in modern cookery is to be regretted.

CRÈMES, SOUFFLÉS, JELLIES, SALADS

Even the simplest meal becomes a feast if crowned with a
delicious sweet course. A sweet tooth is not the prerogative of
the young in years only, and such ingredients as fruit, nuts,
curd cheese, honey or cream are rich in vitamins as well as
appealing to the palate. Especially in summer there is nothing
more refreshing than a bowlful of practically any kind of fruit,
lightly sweetened with sugar, sprinkled with oatmeal and lemon
juice and served with sweet or sour cream. The art of presentation should not be neglected and a few pieces of fruit should
always be reserved for a garnish. If calories do not have to be
counted too carefully, whipped cream can provide the finishing
touch, or be offered separately. The possibilities are endless, so
let your imagination take the lead.

Fruit Cup Piedmont
(PIEMONTER FRUCHTSCHALE)

Ingredients: Bunch of rhubarb, sugar, rind of ½ lemon, ½–¾ lb. (250–375 g.) strawberries, ¼ pt. (⅛ l.) yogurt, condensed or fresh milk.

Prepare the rhubarb, cut into small pieces, simmer with sugar and lemon rind until tender. When cold, pour off some of the syrup. Wash and slice the strawberries and combine with the rhubarb. Mix a little milk with the yogurt and pour over the fruit.

Mixed Fruit Salad
(BUNTE FRUCHTSCHÜSSEL)

Ingredients: ½ lb. (250 g.) rhubarb, 2–3 bananas, 2 oranges, few strawberries, sugar, vanilla sugar, flaked almonds.

Clean and shred the rhubarb. Chop the other fruits and mix in a bowl. Sweeten with sugar and vanilla sugar and garnish with almonds.

Serve with whipped cream if desired.

Swabian Rhubarb
(SCHWÄBISCHE RHABARBERSPEISE)

Ingredients: 1 lb. (500 g.) rhubarb, rind of 1 lemon, 8 oz. (250 g.) sugar, ¾–1 pt. (½ l.) milk, 2 oz. (60 g.) semolina, salt, 1 egg yolk, butter.

Prepare the rhubarb, cut up and cook with 1¾ ounces (50 grammes) sugar, the lemon rind and a very little water. This makes a thick compote. Cook the semolina in the milk with the remaining sugar and a pinch of salt. When thick, remove from the heat and stir in a knob of butter and the egg yolk. Remove the lemon rind and mix together the fruit and semolina.

Serve with chocolate sauce.

Rhubarb Pudding Irene
(RHABARBERPUDDING IRENE)

Ingredients: 1¼ lb. (500 g.) rhubarb, rind of ½ lemon, 1 oz. (30 g.) grated almonds or hazelnuts, 5¼ oz. (150 g.) sugar, 2 leaves gelatine (1 white, 1 red), 7 oz. (200 g.) redcurrants.

Prepare the rhubarb, chop and simmer in ½ pint (¼ litre) water with the lemon rind until tender. Remove lemon rind. Dissolve the gelatine in a little water then fold into the rhubarb together with the almonds and sugar. Turn into a mould and chill. When set turn out and garnish with redcurrants. Serve with vanilla custard or whipped cream.

Flaming Cherries
(BRENNENDE KIRSCHEN)

Ingredients: 1 lb. (500 g.) black cherries, sugar, brandy.

Wash the cherries, stone and remove stalks. Sweeten and arrange on a dish. Pour the brandy over and set alight.

An easily prepared sweet dish and one which never fails to impress.

Fruit in Orange Baskets
(FRÜCHTE IM APFELSINENKÖRBCHEN)

Ingredients: 4 oranges, 8 oz. (250 g.) cherries, brandy, 1 pkt. (1½ tbsp.) vanilla sugar, sugar.

With a sharp knife, cut the skins of the oranges in such a way that you get baskets with handles. Carefully remove the flesh, chop and mix with stoned cherries. Add sugar, vanilla sugar and brandy and fill the baskets with the mixture.

Other fruit can be used instead of cherries.

Morello Jelly from Grandmother's Cookbook
(WEICHSELSULZE)

Pound a quantity of morello cherries in a mortar. Put flesh, stones and juice into a pan, together with lemon rind, cinnamon and sugar to taste. Add deer's horn jelly (grind half a pound of deer's horn, wash carefully, boil in water until reduced to half, strain, reduce liquid further and use as jelly), boil up with egg white until clarified and strain through a cloth. Leave the jelly to set and serve cold or use for decorating cakes etc.

Cherry Delight
(KÖSTLICHE KIRSCHENCREME)

Ingredients: 1 lb. (500 g.) cherries, 2½ oz. (60–80 g.) shredded hazelnuts, 1 tbsp. grated chocolate, ¼ pt. (⅛ l.) cream, sugar.

Wash and stone the cherries, sugar and put aside for ½ hour. Pour the cream over and sprinkle with chocolate and hazelnuts.

Cherries in Wine Jelly
(KIRSCHEN IN WEINGELEE)

Ingredients: 8 oz. (250 g.) sugar, grated rind of ½ lemon, 14 leaves gelatine (12 white, 2 red), ¾ pt. (⅜ l.) white wine, 1 lb. (500 g.) cherries, ¼ pt. (⅛ l.) double cream.

Put the sugar in a pan with the grated lemon rind and a scant ½ pint (¼ litre) water. Bring to the boil, remove from the heat and add the wine. Soak the gelatine in cold water, squeeze it out and add it, when dissolved, to the wine mixture in a double saucepan. Rinse a mould with cold water, put in the stoned cherries and top with the jelly. Unmould just before serving and top with whipped cream.

This recipe is suitable for peaches (8) or apricots. These, however, must be parboiled before being placed in the mould.

Rum Cherries
(RUMKIRSCHEN)

Ingredients: 1 lb. (500 g.) stoned cherries, sugar, 1 small glass rum, ¾–1 pt. (½ l.) milk, 1 pkt. chocolate pudding mix with almonds, dash of rum essence, 1 egg white.

Place the cherries in a bowl, sprinkle them with sugar and pour the rum over. Make a chocolate pudding from the mix, milk and 3½ tablespoons sugar. Add rum essence and fold in the stiffly beaten egg white. Pour the pudding over the fruit and garnish with a few whole cherries.

Cherry Snow
(KIRSCHEN IM SCHNEE)

Ingredients: 1 lb. (500 g.) stoned cherries, sugar, ½ tsp. ground cinnamon, 3 egg whites, grated rind of ½ lemon, ¾–1 oz. (20–30 g.) ground almonds.

Make a purée from the fruit, either in an electric blender or by pounding well in a mortar. Sweeten with sugar and flavour with cinnamon. Add the grated lemon rind and almonds to the stiffly beaten egg whites and combine with the purée.

Serve well chilled.

Romanoff Cup
(ROMANOFF-BECHER)

Ingredients: 8 oz. (250 g.) wild strawberries, 8 oz. (250 g.) garden strawberries, 2 oz. (60 g.) sugar, 1 glass brandy, 4–8 fl. oz. (⅛–¼ l.) double cream.

Hull, wash and rub the wild strawberries through a sieve. Sweeten and chill. Hull and wash the garden strawberries, drain and put a few aside as garnish. Combine the purée with the whole strawberries, add the brandy and arrange in individual glass dishes or champagne glasses. Top with whipped cream and garnish with strawberries.

Crème Surprise

Ingredients: 1½–1¾ lb. (750 g.) strawberries, 3½ oz. (100 g.) sugar, 12 leaves gelatine, 8 fl. oz. (¼ l.) double cream.

Wash and hull the strawberries, put a few aside as garnish. Put the rest through the sieve or the electric blender. Sweeten the purée. Dissolve the gelatine in a little cold water in a double saucepan, stir until smooth and combine with the purée and whipped cream. Rinse a mould or bowl with cold water, fill with fruit cream and chill. Turn out just before serving and decorate with whipped cream and strawberries.

Strawberries in Wine Jelly
(ERDBEEREN IN WEINGELEE)

Ingredients: 13 leaves gelatine (3 white, 10 red), 1¼ pt. (¾ l.)
white wine, 4½ oz. (100–150 g.) sugar, 1½ lb. (500–
750 g.) strawberries, ¼ pt. (⅛ l.) double cream.

Soak the gelatine, squeeze out and dissolve in 1 glass of wine
in a double saucepan. Sweeten the rest of the wine and stir the
gelatine mixture into it. Rinse a pudding mould with cold
water. Cover the bottom to about ½ inch with the wine jelly.
Wash, hull and sprinkle the strawberries with sugar. Put them
into the mould and cover with the remaining jelly, or arrange
alternate layers of fruit and jelly. Chill. Turn out when set
and decorate with whipped cream and strawberries. For additional effect, the strawberries may be dipped in chocolate
icing.

Strawberries with Snow Peaks
(SCHNEEHAUBENSPEISE)

Ingredients: 1 lb. (500 g.) strawberries, 1 small glass brandy,
sugar, 4–8 fl. oz. (⅛–¼ l.) double cream, 2–3 leaves
gelatine, 1½ oz. (30–50 g.) ground almonds or
hazelnuts.

Wash and hull the strawberries, sprinkle first with sugar, then
with brandy and arrange on individual dishes. Soak the gelatine, squeeze it out and dissolve in a double saucepan. Combine
with whipped cream and almonds or hazelnuts. Arrange on top
of the strawberries.

Salad Napoli
(SALAT NAPOLI)

Ingredients: 4 oranges, 1–1¼ lb. (500 g.) strawberries, sugar,
¼ pt. (⅛ l.) cream.

Peel and chop the oranges and hull, wash and drain the strawberries. Mix the fruits, add sugar to taste and combine with
the cream. Chill, decorate with strawberry leaves and serve.

110

Strawberries Ursula
(URSULINENSPEISE)

Ingredients: ¾–1 pt. (½ l.) strong tea, juice of 1 lemon, sugar, 7 leaves white gelatine, 8 oz. (250 g.) strawberries, 1 egg white, icing sugar.

Flavour the tea with lemon juice and sweeten with sugar. Soak the gelatine in water, squeeze out, stir with 1 teaspoon water in a double saucepan until smooth and add to the tea. Hull, wash and chop the strawberries and fold in. Rinse cups with cold water, fill with the fruit mixture and chill. Turn out when set. Beat the egg white stiffly, sweeten with icing sugar and use to decorate the jellies. Garnish each with a whole strawberry.

Raspberries may be used in the same way.

Cheese Cream Brigitte
(QUARKCREME BRIGITTE)

Ingredients: 9 oz. (250 g.) cream cheese, 3½ tbsp. sugar, 2 egg yolks, grated rind of ½ lemon, ¼ pt. (⅛ l.) double cream, 3½ oz. (100 g.) sponge cakes, brandy, 3½ oz. (100 g.) strawberries or raspberries, 2 pineapple rings.

Cream the cheese with the sugar and egg yolks and flavour with grated lemon rind and brandy. Prepare and chop the fruit and fold in together with the whipped cream. Soak the sponge cakes with a little brandy, line a dish with them and fill with the cream mixture.

A delicious dish.

Strawberry Dream
(ERDBEER-TRAUMSPEISE)

Ingredients: 1 lb. (500 g.) strawberries, 3–4 egg whites, 3½ tbsp. icing sugar, 5–7 tbsp. thick sour cream, grated rind of ½ lemon, 1 pkt. (1½ tbsp.) vanilla sugar.

Wash and hull the strawberries, halve and sweeten with vanilla sugar. Beat the egg whites stiffly, add the icing sugar, grated lemon rind and fold in the beaten sour cream. Place the fruit

111

in a bowl and top with the cream mixture. Serve at once. More sugar or vanilla sugar may be added if desired.

Viennese Strawberry Cups
(WIENER ERDBEERCOUPÉ)

Ingredients: ¾–1 pt. (½ l.) milk, ½ vanilla pod, 1 oz. (30 g.) sugar, ½ oz. (15 g.) potato flour, 2 egg yolks, rum essence, 3–4 leaves gelatine, 8 oz. (200–250 g.) strawberries, 8 fl. oz. (¼ l.) double cream, grated chocolate.

Bring the milk to the boil with the sugar and vanilla pod. Mix the potato flour with a little water and the yolks, add to the milk and boil up a few times, beating continuously. Add a few drops of rum essence. Dissolve the gelatine in a double saucepan in the usual way and fold into the whipped cream. Combine the milk mixture and cream. Finally, add the hulled, washed and halved strawberries. Serve in glass dishes, sprinkled with grated chocolate.

The dish can be prepared without the whipped cream.

Strawberry Soufflé Monte Carlo
(ERDBEERSOUFFLÉ MONTE CARLO)

Ingredients: 1½–1¾ lb. (750 g.) strawberries, 2 oz. (50–60 g.) sugar, 5 eggs, 1 glass brandy, rum or cherry brandy, butter, breadcrumbs.

Wash, hull and chop the strawberries, put in a dish and sprinkle with a little sugar. Pour over the brandy or rum and leave for 30 minutes. Separate the eggs. Beat the yolks with the sugar and fold in the stiffly beaten whites. Butter a soufflé dish, sprinkle with breadcrumbs and put in the strawberries with the egg mixture on top. Alternatively, the fruit and egg mixture may be mixed before putting it in the dish. Bake in a moderate oven for 10–15 minutes.

Strawberries with Chocolate
(ERDBEEREN IM SCHOKOLADENMANTEL)

Ingredients: 9–10 oz. (250–300 g.) large ripe strawberries, 3 oz. (2 pkt.) chocolate icing.

Wash the strawberries, place on a sieve to drain and dry with a soft cloth. Dissolve the icing in a double saucepan and, holding the stalk carefully, dip each strawberry in the chocolate. When coated, place the strawberries on a plate and chill in the refrigerator.

Garnished Redcurrant Cream
(GARNIERTER JOHANNISBEERSCHAUM)

Ingredients: 3 egg whites, 1 lb. (500 g.) redcurrants, sugar, peach halves or pineapple rings.

Beat the whites stiffly and fold in the sugar-dusted redcurrants. Place in individual dishes and decorate with peach halves or pineapple rings.

Fruit Cream Astoria
(FRUCHTCREME ASTORIA)

Ingredients: 8 oz. (250 g.) gooseberries, 8 oz. (250 g.) redcurrants, 3½ oz. (125 g.) sugar, lemon rind, 9–10 leaves gelatine per pt. (½ l.) fruit juice, 2 egg whites.

Prepare and wash the fruit, cook with the sugar and lemon rind and rub through a sieve. Soak the gelatine, stir in a double saucepan until smooth and add to the fruit juice. When the mixture is beginning to set, fold in the stiffly beaten egg whites. Chill. Garnish with a few redcurrants and serve with vanilla custard.

Redcurrants with Cream Cheese
(JOHANNISBEERQUARKSCHALE)

Ingredients: 1 lb. (500 g.) redcurrants, sugar, 1 pkt. (1½ tbsp.) vanilla sugar, 8 oz. (250 g.) cream cheese.

Make a compote from the redcurrants with sugar and a little water. Cool, flavour with vanilla sugar and combine with the beaten cheese.

Blackcurrants or other kinds of fruit may be used for this dish. If blackcurrants are used they should be rubbed through a sieve before flavouring. Curd cheese may be used instead of cream cheese.

Quick Gooseberry Cream
(STACHELBEER-BLITZCREME)

Ingredients: 1 lb. (500 g.) gooseberries, rind of 1 lemon, piece of cinnamon stick, 3¼ oz. (100 g.) sugar, 1 glass white wine, 3 eggs.

Prepare and wash the gooseberries. Make a compote, adding lemon rind, cinnamon and sugar. Drain, combine the juice with the wine and egg yolks and beat over a low heat until the cream begins to thicken. Fold in the stiffly beaten whites, add the gooseberries and serve with biscuits.

Gooseberry Jellies
(STACHELBEERKÖPFCHEN)

Ingredients: 1–1¼ lb. (500 g.) gooseberries, 2–3 leaves gelatine, 5–7 tbsp. sugar, ¼–½ pt. (⅛–¼ l.) yogurt.

Prepare, wash and cook the gooseberries and rub them through a sieve. Soak the gelatine, squeeze out and stir with 1 teaspoon of water in a double saucepan until smooth. Combine with the sweetened fruit juice. Rinse cups with cold water, fill with the mixture and leave in the refrigerator to set. Turn out the jellies and serve with a topping of yogurt.

Fruit Charlotte
(FRÜCHTE-CHARLOTTE)

Ingredients: 1½–1¾ lb. (750 g.) redcurrants or gooseberries, 7 oz. (200 g.) sugar, 1 stick cinnamon, piece of butter, sponge cake or biscuits, condensed milk or milk with vanilla sugar.

Prepare and wash the fruit, add the sugar, cinnamon and with very little water prepare a thick compote. Rub through a sieve. Add beaten butter and more sugar if desired. Line a glass dish neatly with piece of sponge cake or biscuits and pour in the fruit juice. Cover with a layer of cake or biscuits. Chill for several hours. Turn out when set and serve with milk to which vanilla sugar has been added or with condensed milk.

Other kinds of fruit may be used in the same way.

Gooseberry Cream Limburg
(LIMBURGER STACHELBEERCREME)

Ingredients: 1–1¼ lb. (500 g.) gooseberries, ¾ oz. (20 g.) potato
flour, sugar, 1 oz. (20–30 g.) hazelnuts, 2–3 egg
whites, condensed milk or sour cream.

Wash and prepare the fruit and cook in 1¾ pints (1 litre) water
until tender. Sieve and thicken the resulting juice with potato
flour. Add sugar and continue to stir, off the heat. Add
chopped hazelnuts and fold in the stiffly beaten egg whites.
Chill and serve with condensed milk or sour cream.

This is an all seasons dish which can be prepared from
bottled gooseberries.

Yogurt Carina
(JOGHURTSPEISE KARINA)

Ingredients: ½ pt. (¼ l.) yogurt, 3½ tbsp. sugar, juice and grated
rind of ½ lemon, 6 leaves white gelatine, 8 oz.
(250 g.) raspberries.

Beat together the yogurt, sugar and lemon juice and grated
rind. Soak the gelatine, dissolve in a double saucepan and add
to the yogurt together with the raspberries which have been
puréed with a fork. Leave in refrigerator until firm. Garnish
with raspberries.

Raspberry Pudding Antoinette
(HIMBEERPUDDING ANTOINETTE)

Ingredients: 1½–1¾ lb. (750 g.) raspberries, 3 oz. (80 g.) sugar,
3 leaves gelatine, 2 oz. (50 g.) sponge cake or
biscuits, brandy or rum.

Rub the raspberries through a sieve, sweeten the purée and
combine with the gelatine which has been softened and dissolved in a double saucepan. Rinse a round bowl or pudding
basin with cold water and put in a layer of sponge cake or biscuits. Sprinkle with rum or brandy and put a layer of raspberry
purée on top. Continue with alternate layers of cake and fruit
until all are used. Put the dish in the refrigerator. When set,
turn out, and serve garnished with raspberries. If the pudding

has been prepared in a glass dish it can be served directly from the dish.

Raspberry Baisers
(HIMBEER-BAISERS)

Ingredients: 1 lb. (500 g.) raspberries, 2 oz. (50–60 g.) sugar, 3 egg whites, 3½–5 tbsp. icing sugar.

Put the cleaned and sugared raspberries into a heatproof dish. Beat the whites stiffly, stir in the icing sugar and distribute the mixture over the fruit. Bake for 3–5 minutes in a hot oven until the meringue turns golden brown. Serve at once.

Mirabelle Soufflé
(MIRABELLENSOUFFLÉ)

Ingredients: 1 lb. (500 g.) Mirabelle plums, butter, bread-crumbs, ¾ oz. (20 g.) blanched almonds, 7 oz. (200 g.) sugar, 1½ oz. (40 g.) butter, 1½ oz. (40 g.) flour, 3 eggs, scant ½ pt. (¼ l.) milk.

Wash and stone the plums and poach in a very little water with about half the sugar. Butter a heatproof dish, sprinkle with breadcrumbs and put in the fruit. Melt the butter in a pan, stir in the flour and add the milk. Continue to cook until the mixture thickens. Take the pan off the heat and add the remaining sugar, shredded almonds and egg yolks. Finally, fold in the stiffly beaten whites, pour the mixture over the fruit and bake in a medium oven for 30–35 minutes. The oven should not be opened during the first 25 minutes to prevent the soufflé from collapsing.

Egg plums or greengages can be used in the same way.

Apricot Flummery
(APRIKOSENFLAMMERI)

Ingredients: 1 lb. (500 g.) fresh or tinned apricots, 2½–5 tsp. brandy, 2 pkt. (3 tbsp.) vanilla sugar, 1 egg, 3½ tbsp. sugar, 1½ oz. (40 g.) potato flour, grated lemon rind, ¾–1 pt. (½ l.) milk, 2–3 tbsp. ground hazelnuts.

Place the apricots in hot water, lift out and skin. Stone and slice the fruit, place in a glass dish and sprinkle with vanilla sugar and brandy. Beat the egg yolk with sugar, add grated lemon rind, potato flour and a little milk and stir until smooth. Bring the remaining milk to the boil and add the mixture, stirring continuously. Take the pan off the heat and fold in the stiffly beaten egg white. Arrange over the fruit and serve with a garnish of hazelnuts mixed with vanilla sugar.

The brandy may be left out if preferred.

Cream Stefanie
(STEFANIE-CREME)

Ingredients: 6 apricots or 4 peaches, 8 oz. (250 g.) cream cheese, $3\frac{1}{2}$ tbsp. sugar, 1 pkt. ($1\frac{1}{2}$ tbsp.) vanilla sugar, rum essence, $\frac{1}{2}$ pt. ($\frac{1}{4}$ l.) double cream, 1 egg white, grated coconut or whipped cream.

Wash and stone the fruit and put through the blender or mash with a fork, blanching and chopping the fruit first. Combine the fruit purée with the cream cheese, flavour with sugar, vanilla sugar and rum essence and finally fold in the whipped cream and stiffly beaten egg white. Serve in glass dishes, garnished with grated coconut or whipped cream.

Apricot Dessert
(APRIKOSENDESSERT)

Ingredients: $1\frac{1}{2}$–$1\frac{3}{4}$ lb. (750 g.) apricots or peaches, $2\frac{1}{2}$–3 oz. (80 g.) sugar, 1 pkt. ($1\frac{1}{2}$ tbsp.) vanilla sugar, rum essence, 1 egg white.

Blanch and stone the fruit and chop one half very finely. Make a purée of the remainder, combine with the chopped fruit, add sugar and flavourings and fold in the stiffly beaten egg white. Serve at once.

Apricot Jellies
(APRIKOSENKÖPFCHEN)

Ingredients: $1\frac{1}{2}$ lb. (500–700 g.) apricots, juice of 1 lemon, $3\frac{1}{2}$ oz. (100 g.) sugar, 4 leaves gelatine (2 white, 2 red), $1\frac{3}{4}$ oz. (50 g.) shredded almonds.

Halve the apricots, remove the stones and cook in water until tender. Rub the fruit through a sieve. The resulting juice should amount to about 1¾ pints (1 litre). Stir in the lemon juice and sugar. Soak the gelatine, squeeze out and dissolve in 2–3 teaspoons water in a double saucepan. Use to thicken the fruit juice. Leave to cool. Rinse a few cups with cold water, sprinkle with shredded almonds and fill with the jelly mixture. Turn out when set and decorate each jelly with half an apricot. Serve with vanilla custard or whipped cream.

Iced Peaches
(GEEISTE PFIRSICHE)

Ingredients: ½ peach per person, 4–7 oz. (125–200 g.) raspberries, sugar, 1 pkt. (1½ tbsp.) vanilla sugar, lemon juice, 8 fl. oz. (¼ l.) double cream.

Blanch the peaches, remove skins, halve and stone. Roll each half in sugar which has been flavoured with vanilla sugar and sprinkle with lemon juice. Fill the freezer tray of the refrigerator with whipped cream and place the peach halves on top. Put into freezer compartment and freeze until quite firm. Serve on individual plates and garnish with raspberries.

Apricots, cherries, strawberries or pineapple may be used in the same way, and vanilla custard may be substituted for the double cream.

Crowned Peaches
(KRONEN-PFIRSICHE)

Ingredients: 3 large and juicy peaches, sugar, 1 pkt. (1½ tbsp.) vanilla sugar, 1½ oz. (40 g.) shredded almonds, 1 egg, butter, juice of 1 lemon, 1–2 glasses white wine.

Blanch and skin the peaches, halve two and purée the third. Sweeten the purée, flavour with vanilla sugar and stir in the almonds and egg yolk. Fill the peach halves with the purée mixture and place in a buttered heatproof dish. Sprinkle with lemon juice, pour over the wine and bake in a moderate oven for 10 minutes. Whisk the egg whites very stiffly, pile on top of the peaches and return to the oven for a few more minutes.

Fruit Flambés
(FLAMBIERTE FRÜCHTE)

Ingredients: 2 bananas, 4 peaches, 2 oz. (60 g.) butter, 1 glass
rum or brandy, 3½ tbsp. sugar, ¼ pt. (⅛ l.) cream,
2–3 tbsp. any fruit juice or white wine.

Melt the butter in a copper pan or an electric heater at the
table, or on the stove. Peel and halve the bananas, skin and
chop the peaches. Place the fruit in the pan, sprinkle with
sugar and pour over the brandy or rum. Set alight and cover
the pan until the flames have died. Put the fruit, without the
juice, on warm plates. Pour the cream into the pan and add
fruit juice or white wine if available. Simmer the mixture for
2 minutes, pour over the fruit and serve this delicious sweet at
once.

Pineapple rings or the same amount of fruit salad can be
used in the same way. Watching the preparation of their sweet
dish at the table is sure to delight your guests.

Baked Peaches
(ÜBERBACKENE PFIRSICHE)

Ingredients: 2 large peaches, 2 oz. (50 g.) ground almonds,
1½–2 tbsp. white wine, 1 pkt. (1½ tbsp.) vanilla
sugar, grated rind of 1 lemon, 3½ tbsp. sugar, 2
egg whites.

Halve the fruit, remove the stones and place them, cut side up,
in a heatproof dish. Sprinkle with wine. Mix together the
sugar, vanilla sugar, grated lemon rind and almonds and fold
in the stiffly beaten whites. Top the fruit with teaspoonfuls of
the mixture, bake in a moderate oven for 5 minutes and grill
for a further 5 minutes. Serve hot or cold.

Apricots may be used in the same way.

Peach Cream
(PFIRSICHSCHAUM)

Ingredients: 4–6 large peaches, 1–2 pkt. (1½–3 tbsp.) vanilla
sugar, sugar, 8 fl. oz. (¼ l.) double cream.

Wash and stone the fruit and purée either in the blender or by rubbing through a sieve. Sweeten to taste with sugar and vanilla sugar and fold in the whipped cream.

This cream holds its shape better if 2 leaves gelatine, dissolved in a double saucepan in the usual way, are stirred into the purée or the cream before combining.

Simple Peach Dessert
(EINFACHE PFIRSICHSPEISE)

Ingredients: 4 large and ripe peaches, juice of 1½ lemons, 1 pkt. (1½ tbsp.) vanilla sugar, 1¾ oz. (50 g.) sugar.

Blanch, skin, halve the fruit and remove the stones. Sprinkle with lemon juice, roll in a mixture of sugar and vanilla sugar and serve, cut side downwards, on glass dishes.

Peach Pudding
(PFIRSICH-PUDDING)

Ingredients: 2–2¼ lb. (1 kg.) peaches, 1¾ oz. (50 g.) sugar, grated rind and juice of 1 lemon, 15 leaves gelatine (10 white, 5 red), 2 oz. (60 g.) almonds.

Peel, halve and stone the peaches. Put two aside as garnish and poach the rest with the sugar and grated lemon rind in a little water. Rub the fruit through a sieve. Add the lemon juice. Soak the gelatine in a little water, squeeze out, dissolve in a double saucepan and stir into the purée. Rinse a mould with cold water, add the blanched and chopped almonds to the pudding mixture and pour into the mould. Turn out and garnish with peach slices. Serve with vanilla custard.

Peaches Ligurian Style
(LIGURISCHE PFIRSICHSPEISE)

Ingredients: 5 large peaches, 1¾ oz. (50 g.) biscuit crumbs, 1 pkt. (1½ tbsp.) vanilla sugar, 2–3 tbsp. sugar, brandy, ¼–½ pt. (¼ l.) red wine.

Blanch, skin and stone the peaches. Mash one peach with a fork, combine the purée with the biscuit crumbs and flavour with brandy. Fill the halves with the purée and place them in a heatproof dish. Sprinkle with vanilla sugar and sugar. Pour the wine over the fruit and bake in a moderate oven.

Cranberry Snow
(PREISELBERRSHNEE)

Ingredients: 3 egg whites, 3½ tbsp. icing sugar, ½ pt. (¼ l.) cranberry compote.

Beat the whites stiffly, folding in icing sugar and fruit.

Hidden Blackberries
(VERDECKTE BROMBEEREN)

Ingredients: 1 lb. (500 g.) blackberries, 8 oz. (250 g.) curd cheese, condensed milk, 1¾ oz. (50 g.) grated hazelnuts, 2 oz. (60 g.) sugar, 1 egg white, 1 pkt. (1½ tbsp.) vanilla sugar.

Prepare the blackberries, place in a bowl and sprinkle with sugar. Beat the cheese with condensed milk, add first the hazelnuts, then fold in the stiffly beaten egg white and flavour with sugar and vanilla sugar. Pile the mixture on top of the fruit and serve with sweet biscuits.

The cheese mixture (without the beaten egg white) may be used as a stuffing for large halved strawberries. An attractive sweet for special occasions.

Bilberry Jelly with Yogurt
(JOGHURT-HEIDELBEERSÜLZE)

Ingredients: ½ pt. (¼ l.) yogurt, 3½ oz. (100 g.) sugar, grated rind of ½ lemon, 6–7 leaves gelatine, 8 oz. (250 g.) bilberries.

Flavour the yogurt with the sugar and grated lemon rind and beat well. Soak the gelatine, squeeze out, dissolve in a double saucepan in ¾ tablespoon water and combine with the yogurt. Prepare, wash and drain the bilberries and add to the yogurt. Chill, and serve when set, with vanilla custard or fruit sauce if desired.

Other soft fruits may be served in the same way.

Garnished Apples
(ZWIEBACKÄPFEL)

Ingredients: 6 round rusks, 3 large apples, ¼ pt. (⅛ l.) white
wine, sugar, ½ stick cinnamon, 1 piece lemon or
orange rind, ¼ pt. (⅛ l.) double cream, redcurrant
jelly.

Peel and halve the apples, remove the cores and poach them
in the wine, to which the sugar, cinnamon, rind and a little
water have been added. Care must be taken not to overcook
the apples which should retain their shape. Lift the fruit on to
a dish and continue to reduce the syrup by boiling until it is
thick. Arrange the fruit halves on the rusks, coat with the
syrup and decorate with whipped cream and a little redcurrant
jelly, if available.

Bismarck Apples
(BISMARCKÄPFEL)

Ingredients: 4 apples, 2 oz. (60 g.) raisins, sugar, 8 fl. oz. (¼ l.)
cream, 2 egg yolks, 1¾ tsp. potato flour, ¾ oz. (20
g.) sugar, vanilla essence, 2 oz. (60 g.) almonds,
redcurrant jelly.

Peel and halve the apples, remove the cores and poach carefully in a little sweetened water. Arrange the apples on a serving dish and stuff with raisins. Combine the cream, yolks,
potato flour and sugar and beat in a mixing bowl over a saucepan of boiling water until the sauce thickens. Flavour with
vanilla essence and spoon over the fruit. Sprinkle with chopped
almonds and garnish with the jelly. Serve either hot or well
chilled.

Apple Paste Yvonne
(APFELPASTE YVONNE)

Ingredients: 2 lb. (1 kg.) apples, 5 oz. (150 g.) sugar, vanilla
sugar or sugar.

Peel the apples, chop and simmer in a very little water until
soft. Sieve, add the sugar to the purée and cook until very thick.
Spread the paste on a marble slab or porcelain dish and leave

to dry. Cut into diamond shapes, coat with sugar or sprinkle with vanilla sugar. Delicious served with vanilla custard.

Stuffed Apples
(SCHÜSSELOBSTSPEISE)

Ingredients: 4 large apples, juice of 1–2 lemons or a little white wine, 5–7 tbsp. jam or chopped almonds and raisins.

Peel and core the apples. Add a little water to the wine or lemon juice and cook the apples in it over a low heat, taking care to keep them intact. Drain the apples on a sieve and fill the core cavities with jam or almonds and raisins. Arrange the apples on a glass dish and serve with chocolate sauce or vanilla custard.

Another filling is a mixture of fried oatmeal, sugar and raisins.

Apple Cream
(APFEL-QUARKCREME)

Ingredients: ¾ pt. (½ l.) milk, 1 pkt. (2 tbsp.) custard powder, 3½ tbsp. sugar, 8 oz. (250 g.) curd cheese, 6 tbsp. apple purée.

Make a custard, sweeten with the sugar, take it off the heat and stir in the cheese. Whisk well and leave to cool. Combine with the purée. Serve with sweet biscuits.

Paris Apple Dessert
(PARISER APFELDESSERT)

Ingredients: 3–4 cooking apples, butter, sugar, cinnamon, 1–1½ oz. (30–40 g.) raisins, juice of 1 lemon, 1 pt. (½ l.) white wine.

Peel the apples, remove the cores and cut into rings about ¼ inch thick. Fry these in butter on both sides, lift out and sprinkle with sugar and cinnamon. Soak the raisins in luke-warm water. Drain. Arrange the apple rings in a dish with the raisins on top and pour wine and lemon juice over the fruit.

Apple Purée with Meringue
(APFELMUS MIT MERINGUENGUSS)

Ingredients: Purée of $3\frac{1}{4}$ lb. ($1\frac{1}{2}$ kg.) apples, grated lemon rind, vanilla sugar, 2 oz. (60 g.) ground almonds, 3 egg whites, 5 tbsp. icing sugar, pinch of baking powder.

Flavour the purée with grated lemon rind and vanilla sugar, place in a greased pudding basin and sprinkle almonds on top. Stiffly beat the egg whites and mix with icing sugar and baking powder. Spread over the purée and bake in a moderate oven for 5–10 minutes.

Pear Foam
(BIRNENSCHNEE)

Ingredients: 2–$2\frac{1}{4}$ lb. (1 kg.) pears, 2 egg whites, $2\frac{1}{2}$–$3\frac{1}{2}$ oz. (80–100 g.) sugar, 1 pkt. ($1\frac{1}{2}$ tbsp.) vanilla sugar, juice of 1 lemon.

Peel, core and halve the pears and poach in a very little water until tender. Drain and rub through a sieve. Leave to cool. Flavour the purée with vanilla sugar, sugar and lemon juice and fold in the stiffly beaten egg whites. Serve chilled.

Apples can be served in the same way.

Swabian Pear Salad
(SCHWÄBISCHER BIRNENSALAT)

Ingredients: 2–$2\frac{1}{4}$ lb. (1 kg.) pears, sugar, cinnamon, juice of 2 lemons, 1 glass brandy or rum, 1 mandarin orange.

Peel the pears, remove the cores and slice thinly. Sprinkle with sugar and cinnamon. Pour the brandy and lemon juice over the fruit and chill in the refrigerator for several hours. Serve with a garnish of mandarin slices.

Favourite Pears
(FAVORITEN-BIRNEN)

Ingredients: 4 large juicy pears, 1 pkt. ($1\frac{1}{2}$ tbsp.) vanilla sugar, 4 portions vanilla ice cream, $5\frac{1}{2}$ oz. (150 g.) plain chocolate, 1 oz. (30 g.) butter.

Peel and halve the pears. Remove the cores and poach with the vanilla sugar in a little water until tender but not mushy. Melt the chocolate in a pan and stir in the butter. Quickly arrange the ice cream on glass dishes, top with the pear halves, pour over the hot chocolate sauce and serve at once.

Roman Pear Slices
(RÖMISCHE BIRNENSCHEIBEN)

Ingredients: 1–2 juicy pears, 4 oz. (125 g.) thinly sliced Gruyère or Emmenthal cheese.

Peel and halve the pears, remove the cores and slice thinly. Top each pear slice with a slice of cheese and serve.

Combinations of fruit and cheese are favourite dessert dishes in Italy.

Grapes Diabolo
(TRAUBENSPEISE DIABOLO)

Ingredients: 1 lb. (375–500 g.) grapes (mixed colours), juice of 2 oranges and 1 lemon, 5 tbsp. sugar, 2 eggs, ¼ pt. (⅛ l.) double cream.

Combine the juices, sugar and eggs in a double saucepan and beat over hot water until thick. Fold in the whipped cream and serve with the grapes.

Sugared Grapes
(TRAUBEN IM ZUCKERHEMD)

Ingredients: 1½ lb. (500–750 g.) grapes, 2 egg whites, icing sugar.

Prepare, wash and drain the grapes. Coat with egg white first and then thickly with icing sugar.

Merano Grape Dessert
(MERANER TRAUBENDESSERT)

Ingredients: ¾–1 pt. (½ l.) milk, 3½–5 tbsp. sugar, grated rind of 1 lemon, 1 egg, 1¾ oz. (50 g.) potato flour, 8 oz. (250 g.) black grapes, 1 pt. (½ l.) grape or apple juice, double cream.

Mix 1 ounce (30 grammes) potato flour, $3\frac{1}{2}$ tablespoons sugar, the egg yolk and a little milk to a smooth paste. Heat the rest of the milk and stir into the paste. Flavour with grated lemon rind, leave to cool a little, then fold in the stiffly beaten egg white. Thicken the fruit juice with $\frac{3}{4}$ ounce (20 grammes) potato flour, sweeten to taste, add the grapes and leave to cool a little. Put alternate layers of the two mixtures into a glass dish and serve chilled. Decorate with whipped cream.

Bohemian Plum Cream
(BÖHMISCHE PFLAUMENCREME)

Ingredients: 1 lb. (500 g.) plums, sugar, 1 stick cinnamon, 7 oz. (200 g.) curd cheese, $\frac{1}{2}$ pt. ($\frac{1}{4}$ l.) double cream.

Wash, stone and cook the plums with sugar and cinnamon in a little water until tender. Drain and rub through a sieve. Combine the purée with the beaten curd cheese, add sugar if necessary and fold in the whipped cream. Serve in a glass dish and decorate with fresh, sliced plums.

Grecian Plums
(GRIECHISCHE PFLAUMENSCHLEMMEREI)

Ingredients: 7 oz. (200 g.) prunes, equal number blanched almonds, 5 tbsp. honey.

Soak the prunes overnight. Drain, make a slit in each prune, remove the stone and replace with an almond. Heat the honey and dip each prune into it, coating it well. Serve on cocktail sticks as a special dessert.

Dates can be served in the same way.

Orange Soufflé Madeleine
(ORANGEN-SOUFFLÉ MADELEINE)

Ingredients: 2–3 large oranges, $3\frac{1}{2}$ oz. (100 g.) sugar, 2–3 eggs, juice of $\frac{1}{2}$ lemon, $3\frac{1}{2}$ oz. (100 g.) ground hazelnuts, $\frac{3}{4}$ oz. (20 g.) potato flour, butter.

Peel and chop the oranges and place them in a buttered soufflé dish. Cream the sugar with the egg yolks and lemon juice, add the hazelnuts and potato flour, then fold in the stiffly beaten whites. Pile the mixture on top of the oranges and bake in a moderate oven for 25–30 minutes. Serve at once.

Orange Slices Flambés
(ABGEBRANNTE ORANGENSCHEIBEN)

Ingredients: 4–5 oranges, 4–7 oz. (125–200 g.) sugar, brandy, butter.

From equal parts of sugar and water ($\frac{1}{4}$–$\frac{1}{2}$ pint [$\frac{1}{8}$–$\frac{1}{4}$ litre]) make a syrup, then leave it to cool. Peel and slice the oranges, place in the syrup and leave for 20–30 minutes. Transfer the fruit to a buttered heatproof dish and cook in the oven at a low heat for 15–20 minutes. Sprinkle with sugar, bring to the table, pour brandy over the fruit and set alight. Serve as soon as the flames have died down.

Creme Royale
(CREME ROYAL)

Ingredients: 2 eggs, scant $\frac{1}{2}$ pt. ($\frac{1}{4}$ l.) milk, 3 oz. (80 g.) sugar, 1 oz. (30 g.) flour, juice of 3 oranges, biscuits or sponge cakes, $\frac{1}{4}$ pt. ($\frac{1}{8}$ l.) double cream, hazelnuts.

Place the egg yolks, milk, 2 ounces (50 grammes) sugar, flour and the juice of 2 oranges into a saucepan. Beat the ingredients until smooth and bring to the boil gently, stirring constantly. Take off the heat and fold in the stiffly beaten egg whites together with the remaining sugar. Line a glass dish with biscuits or sponge cakes, sprinkle with orange juice and pile in the hot mixture. When cold, garnish with hazelnuts and whipped cream.

Orange Fondue
(ORANGEN-FONDUE)

Ingredients: 8 oranges, 5 oz. (150 g.) sugar, 2 glasses white wine, 4 oz. (125 g.) grated almonds or hazelnuts.

Peel all the oranges. Extract the juice from four of them and finely chop the peel. Heat the sugar in a pan, lower the heat when it colours slightly and pour in the wine and orange juice. Stir well and add the chopped orange peel. Transfer the sauce to a heatproof fondue pot and keep it at boiling point on a spirit lamp at the table. Slice the remaining oranges and place them on one dish, the grated nuts on another. Hand round cocktail sticks. Your guests spear an orange slice and dip it first into the sauce, then into the hazelnuts.

An unusual delicacy which never fails to amuse.

Oranges Milano
(MAILÄNDER ORANGENSPEISE)

Ingredients: 2 oz. (60 g.) flour, 6 eggs, $3\frac{1}{2}$ oz. (100 g.) sugar, juice of 3 oranges, $\frac{1}{4}-\frac{1}{2}$ pt. ($\frac{1}{4}$ l.) apple juice, juice of 1 lemon, sponge cakes, butter, 1 orange.

Make a thick cream from the flour, egg yolks, sugar and fruit juices. Beat the whites stiffly and fold in. Put the mixture in a buttered dish which has been lined with sponge cakes. Bake in a moderate oven until firm and garnish with orange slices.

Orange Jelly à la Muscovite
(ORANGENGELÉE À LA MOSCOVITE)

Ingredients: Grated rind and juice of 2 oranges, 9 oz. (250 g.) sugar, juice of 2 lemons, $1\frac{1}{4}$ pt. ($\frac{3}{4}$ l.) white wine, 20 leaves white gelatine, $2\frac{1}{2}$ tsp. cherry brandy, 1 orange.

Bring the sugar to the boil with a little water and add the grated orange rind. Put aside. Soak the gelatine, squeeze out and dissolve in a double saucepan. Strain the orange and lemon juices and add to the wine, together with the strained sugar solution, the gelatine and the cherry brandy. Rinse a mould with cold water, pour in the jelly mixture and chill in the refrigerator. Serve turned out or in the mould, garnished with orange slices. Serve with buttermilk.

Orange Salad à la Grandmere
(ORANGENSALAT À LA GROSSMAMA)

Ingredients: 4–6 blood oranges, 1 pkt. ($1\frac{1}{2}$ tbsp.) vanilla sugar, 2–3 tbsp. sugar, 3–5 tbsp. rum or brandy, 1 oz. (20–30 g.) pistachio nuts.

Peel the oranges, slice, and sprinkle with sugar, vanilla sugar and rum or brandy. Add the pistachio nuts and leave for an hour or so. Arrange the salad on a glass dish and place a few ice cubes on top. Serve with a bowl of sour cream.

The salad may be served as a first course or as a side dish with meat courses. In this case omit the sugar and pour over double cream seasoned with pepper and salt.

Lemon Jelly with Fruit
(ZITRONENGELÉE MIT FRÜCHTEN)

Ingredients: 5 eggs, 5½ oz. (150 g.) sugar, grated rind and juice of 1 lemon, 9 leaves gelatine, 1½ tbsp. each of raspberries, strawberries, chopped pineapple and peaches.

Beat the egg yolks with the sugar, lemon rind and juice. Soak the gelatine, squeeze out and dissolve in a little hot water. Add to the egg mixture. When it begins to set fold in the stiffly beaten whites and the fruit.

Orange may be used similarly to lemon.

Lemon Cream Petra
(ZITRONENCREME PETRA)

Ingredients: 3 egg whites, 1 egg, 3½ oz. (100 g.) sugar, juice of 1½ lemons.

Beat the egg whites with 1 oz. (30 g.) sugar until stiff. Set aside. Combine the egg and remaining sugar in the top of a double saucepan and beat lightly. Then add the lemon juice and whisk the mixture over hot, but not boiling, water until bubbles begin to form round the edge of the saucepan and the mixture begins to thicken. Take the pan off the stove and fold in the beaten egg whites. Pour the cream into a serving dish and chill. Serve this exquisite cream with sponge biscuits and whipped cream if desired.

Geneva Banana Delight
(GENFER BANANENLECKEREI)

Ingredients: 2–3 bananas, juice of 1 lemon, 1 pkt. (1½ tbsp.) vanilla sugar, ¾ lb. (375 g.) redcurrants, sugar.

Peel the bananas and cut in half lengthwise. Place them on a dish and sprinkle with vanilla sugar and lemon juice. Rub the redcurrants through a sieve, having set aside a few for garnish. Sweeten the redcurrant juice to taste and pour over the bananas. Garnish with whole berries.

Bilberries or blackberries may be used in a similar way.

Bananas with Chocolate Sauce
(BANANEN MIT HEISSER SCHOKOLADENSAUCE)

Ingredients: 2 bananas, juice of 1 lemon, 4 oz. (100 g.) plain chocolate, butter.

Peel the bananas, halve lengthwise and sprinkle with lemon juice. Melt the chocolate in a double saucepan, add a knob of butter (about 1½ ounces [40 g.]) and pour over the fruit. Serve at once.

Banana Salad
(BANANEN-KOMBI-SALAT)

Ingredients: 4 bananas, juice of 1½–2 lemons, 1 small melon, sugar, chopped almonds or hazelnuts, double cream.

Slice the bananas, sprinkle with sugar and lemon juice. Quarter the melon, remove the pips with a silver spoon and carefully remove the flesh. Dice and combine with the banana slices. Chill. Add a little more sugar just before serving. Garnish with almonds or hazelnuts and top with whipped cream, if desired.

Banana Boats
(BANANENSCHIFFCHEN)

Ingredients: 2 bananas, 4 oz. (125 g.) curd cheese, juice of ½ lemon, cranberry compote.

Peel the bananas in such a way that the remaining skin is boat-shaped. Remove the fruit carefully and mash with a fork. Combine with the curd cheese, flavour with lemon juice and fill the boats with the mixture. Garnish with cranberry compote and fix small sticks of wood in both sides to represent oars.

Bavarian Pineapple Cream

(ANANAS-CREME AUF BAYRISCHE ART)

Ingredients: 1 pineapple (about 1 lb. [500 g.]), 5½ oz. (160 g.)
sugar, 2 egg yolks, 5 leaves white gelatine, 8 fl. oz.
(¼ l.) double cream.

Peel the fruit, cut in half lengthwise and remove the core. Cut
one half into 3–6 strips and slice these thinly. Place the slices
in the pan with the sugar in a scant ½ pint (¼ litre) water and
bring to the boil. Take off the heat, cover and leave to stand.
Cut the other half of the pineapple into slices about ⅛ inch
thick, sprinkle with sugar, cover and set aside. Drain the juice
off the cooked pineapple and combine it with the egg yolk and
the gelatine, which has been soaked, squeezed out and dissolved in a double saucepan. Beat the mixture over fast boiling
water until thick. Set aside. When the cream begins to set,
mix in the cooked pineapple and fold in the whipped cream.
Rinse a pudding mould with cold water, pile in the cream and
chill. Turn out and serve garnished with the large pineapple
slices.

A festive dessert for special occasions.

Pineapple with Pears

(ANANAS MIT BIRNEN)

Ingredients: 2 large pears, sugar, juice of 1 lemon, 1 pkt. (1½
tbsp.) vanilla sugar, 4 pineapple rings, ¼ pt. (⅛ l.)
double cream, 1½ tbsp. chopped candied ginger or
lemon peel.

Peel and halve the pears, remove the cores and poach carefully
with sugar, lemon juice and vanilla sugar in a little water. They
should not be mushy. Drain and leave to cool. Arrange each
half on a pineapple ring, hollow side up, and fill with whipped
cream. Sprinkle with the candied ginger or peel.

Coupe Hawaii

(HAWAII-BECHER)

Ingredients: Pineapple pieces or 4–6 rings, 7 oz. (200 g.) cream
cheese, ¼ pt. (⅛ l.) double cream, 1 pkt. (1½ tbsp.)
vanilla sugar, 1 leaf gelatine, glacé cherries or
walnut halves.

Chop the pineapple rings and combine with the cream cheese. Whip the cream and sweeten with vanilla sugar. Soak the gelatine, squeeze out and dissolve in a cup with $\frac{1}{2}$ teaspoon water in a double saucepan. Add the gelatine to the whipped cream and fold this into the cream cheese. Pile into tall glasses and serve garnished with glacé cherries or walnut halves.

Fruit Juice Pudding Bali
(BALINESISCHER FRUCHTSAFTPUDDING)

Ingredients: 1 oz. (25–30 g.) potato flour, $\frac{3}{4}$–1 pt. ($\frac{1}{2}$ l.) fruit juice, 1 coconut, $2\frac{1}{2}$ tsp. brandy, pineapple pieces or jam.

Stir the potato flour into the fruit juice and cook, stirring constantly, until thick. Take off the stove and add the coconut milk and brandy. Chill. Just before serving, decorate with pineapple or jam and sprinkle with grated coconut.

Oriental Fig Dessert
(ORIENTALISCHES FEIGENDESSERT)

Ingredients: 1–2 fresh figs per person, brown sugar, white wine, sultanas.

Wash the figs, sprinkle with brown sugar and place in a small heatproof dish. Pour white wine over (about $\frac{1}{2}$ pint [$\frac{1}{4}$ litre]), scatter sultanas on top and bake in a moderate oven for 8–10 minutes.

Ballach [Arabian Dessert]

Ingredients: 8 oz. (200–250 g.) dates, $\frac{1}{4}$ pt. ($\frac{1}{8}$ l.) double cream.

Stone the dates, chop or put through the electric blender. Mix with whipped cream.

Quince Cream à la Josephine
(QUITTENCREME À LA JOSEPHINE)

Ingredients: 1 lb. (500 g.) quinces, 5–7 oz. (150–200 g.) sugar, lemon rind, white gelatine, 1 liqueur glass brandy, 8 fl. oz. ($\frac{1}{4}$ l.) double cream. macaroons.

Brush the quinces, peel and slice thinly. Remove the hard core and cook with the sugar, lemon rind and a little water until tender. Rub through a sieve. Soak 15–20 leaves gelatine per 1¾ pints (1 litre) purée, squeeze out, dissolve in a little hot water and add to the juice. Add more sugar if necessary, stir in the brandy and fold in the whipped cream. Chill and serve garnished with macaroons.

Tutti Frutti

Ingredients: 2 bananas, juice of 1 grapefruit, 4 pineapple rings, 1 orange, 1 apple, handful of chopped nuts, ¼ pt. (⅛ l.) double cream, vanilla sugar.

Mash the bananas with a fork or slice and flavour with grapefruit juice. Peel and chop the other fruits. Mix all the fruits and chopped nuts, sweeten with vanilla sugar, and serve topped with whipped cream.

Fruit Quartet
(OBST-QUARTETT)

Ingredients: 7 oz. (200 g.) each of redcurrants, gooseberries, stoned cherries and raspberries, 2–3½ oz. (60–100 g.) desiccated coconut, sugar, brandy.

Place the prepared fruit in a dish and sprinkle with sugar and brandy. Mix with the coconut and serve chilled.

Tempo Fruit Cream with Cheese
(TEMPO-FRUCHTCREME MIT QUARK)

Ingredients: 1 lb. (500 g.) fruit (strawberries, raspberries, redcurrants, blackberries, oranges, pineapple or bananas), sugar, 1 pkt. (1½ tbsp.) vanilla sugar, 8 oz. (250 g.) cream or curd cheese, 1½–2 tbsp. milk.

Prepare the fruit and chop as required. Sprinkle with sugar and vanilla sugar and set aside. Beat the cheese with the milk, then carefully combine with the fruit. Garnish with a few berries and serve chilled.

This dessert can be prepared all year round with any fruit in season.

Fruit Salad Bali
(OBSTSALAT BALI)

Ingredients: 2 oz. (50 g.) mixed candied lemon and orange peel,
2 oz. (50 g.) walnuts, 1 oz. (25 g.) almonds, 2 oz.
(50 g.) dates, 1 oz. (25 g.) raisins, 1 oz. (25 g.) sultanas, 2 apples, 2 oranges, 2 large bananas, 3
sponge cakes, sugar, cherry brandy or brandy.

Shred the candied peel. Blanch, skin and chop the walnuts
and almonds. Stone and quarter the dates. Wash the raisins
and sultanas. Peel and slice the apples, oranges and bananas,
sweeten and sprinkle with brandy. Mix the dried fruits and
candied peel well together. Put alternate layers of these and
the mixed fresh fruit into a glass dish, interspersed with layers
of crumbled sponge cakes. Sprinkle each layer with brandy.
Garnish with nuts and almonds, cover and set aside for an
hour or so before serving.

Ice Cream
(EISCREME)

Ingredients: 2 oz. (50 g.) fruit (strawberries, raspberries or
bananas), brandy, sugar, 1 pt. ($\frac{1}{2}$ l.) coconut milk,
2–3 tbsp. grated chocolate, grated coconut or handful of fruit.

Wash the fruit, mash with a fork or put through the blender.
Sweeten to taste, add some brandy and leave for 10 minutes.
Stir in the coconut milk. Fill the freezing tray with the mixture
and put into the freezing compartment of the refrigerator for a
few hours. When frozen, garnish with grated chocolate and
coconut, berries or banana slices.

Condensed milk can be used instead of coconut milk.

Cream Figaro
(FIGAROCRÈME)

Ingredients: 1$\frac{1}{2}$ lb. (500–750 g.) fruit (soft fruit, oranges, pineapple or bananas), 1 pt. ($\frac{1}{2}$ l.) double cream, 2 egg
yolks, 2–3 tbsp. sugar, 1 pkt. (1$\frac{1}{2}$ tbsp.) vanilla
sugar, 1$\frac{3}{4}$ tsp. potato flour.

Prepare the fruit, chop if necessary, and arrange in a glass dish. Beat the other ingredients over hot water in a double saucepan to a thick cream and serve with the fruit.

In winter, well drained tinned fruit may be used in the same way.

Tipsy Fruit Salad
(BESCHWIPSTER OBSTSALAT)

Ingredients: 1½–1¾ lb. (750 g.) any fruit (soft fruit, plums, oranges, bananas, etc.), shredded almonds, 1 pkt. (1½ tbsp.) vanilla sugar, sugar, 1 glass brandy, double cream.

Prepare and chop the fruit. Add the almonds, sprinkle with sugar and vanilla sugar, mix well together and flavour with the brandy. Set aside for a few hours. Top with whipped cream if desired. Serve with sponge cakes.

Fruit Meringue
(ÜBERBACKENES FRUCHT-DESSERT)

Ingredients: 3 bananas, 1 lb. (500 g.) strawberries, 1 small tin pineapple pieces, ¼ pt. (⅛ litre) white wine or juice of 2–3 lemons, 5–6 egg whites, icing sugar, butter.

Peel and slice the bananas, sprinkle with lemon juice or white wine and set aside for 20–30 minutes. Stiffly beat the egg whites and combine with icing sugar. Put the banana slices into a buttered heatproof dish with some of the meringue mixture. Top with the halved strawberries and pineapple and pile on the rest of the meringue mixture. Bake in a cool oven for 10–15 minutes.

Melon Aphrodite
(MELONE APHRODITE)

Ingredients: 1 medium-sized melon, 8 oz. (250 g.) white grapes, 2 bananas, 8 oz. (250 g.) plums, sugar, 2 glasses white wine or 1 glass brandy, chopped almonds or pistachio nuts.

Halve the melon and remove seeds. Remove the flesh carefully with a silver spoon and dice. Wash and drain the grapes, halve and stone the plums, peel and slice the bananas. Mix the fruits in a dish, sweeten to taste, flavour with wine or brandy and chill. Just before serving transfer the salad to the melon shells and garnish with chopped almonds or pistachio nuts if desired.

Candydies [Candied Fruit on Skewers]
(KANDIERTE OBSTSPIESSCHEN)

Ingredients: 1½ lb. (750 g.) fruit (e.g. cherries, strawberries, white or purple grapes, orange quarters, pineapple pieces, walnut halves), 1½ lb. (750 g.) sugar, wooden skewers.

Impale 4–5 pieces of fruit which have been washed, well drained or dried with a cloth, on each skewer. If using cherries, these must be stoned first. The number of fruits on the skewer depends on its length but about 1 inch on each end should remain free. Walnut halves between the pieces of fruit are delicious; skewering these, however, must be done with particular care because of their brittleness. Now prepare the sugar solution: place the sugar in a small, aluminium pan together with ¼ pint (⅛ litre) water and bring to the boil, stirring constantly; cook for a few minutes, then take off the fire. Dip the prepared skewers into the syrup and turn until well coated. Lay them across a small dish to allow the surplus syrup to drain off. Arrange the candydies on a glass dish. To prevent the sugar from darkening and crystallizing, rinse the pan with cold water first.

If the candied fruit is intended for storing the sugar must be allowed to boil until it thickens (check with a spoon first). Place the prepared fruit in the sugar and leave for several hours. Lift the fruit out and put on a sieve to drain. Bring the sugar solution to the boil again and cook until a thin thread forms when a little of the liquid is lifted out with a spoon. Take the pan off the stove, return the fruit to the syrup and leave to cool. Drain again and repeat the process until the syrup thickens further. Now immerse the fruit in the sugar for the last time; it should cling firmly to the fruit and form a white layer. Should you be unlucky and the sugar does not sufficiently crystallize, do not despair; lift the fruit on to a wooden board or marble slab and leave to dry for a day. Boil the sugar once more, taking care that no bubbles show on the surface (should this occur add a little water). Test again with a spoon to see whether a thread is forming. The process is completed when the sugar adheres to the fruit completely without dripping.

This recipe may require time and a little patience, but the product equals the shopbought variety in quality and is far less expensive.

Stuffed Figs
(GEFÜLLTE FEIGEN)

Ingredients: 1 pkt. (4½ oz. [150 g.]) dried figs, 4 oz. (100–150 g.) cream cheese, 1 oz. (30 g.) shredded almonds, 1 pkt. (1½ tbsp.) vanilla sugar.

Combine the cream cheese with the almonds and flavour with vanilla sugar. Cut the figs in half and pile in a teaspoonful of the cheese mixture. Put a cocktail stick through the fruit. This is a delicacy popular in the Middle East.

Fruit on Skewers
(OBSTSPIESSCHEN)

Ingredients: 3 oranges, 1 banana, pineapple pieces or 2–3 rings, 4 oz. (125 g.) each white and black grapes, 5 oz. (150 g.) Gruyère cheese, plastic or wooden skewers.

Peel 1 orange and the banana and slice, but not too thinly. Dice the pineapple and cheese. Now, stick your skewer first through a slice of orange, then a piece of pineapple, a banana slice, a cube of cheese, and finally a grape. Halve the remaining oranges and stick 3 or more skewers into each half. Serve on glass dishes.

A cherry or a piece of apple may be substituted for the grape. The contents of the skewers may be varied according to season or personal tastes. A savoury variation on this theme can be achieved by combining apple cubes, sprinkled with lemon juice, with herring or anchovy fillets and small pieces of lemon (skin removed).

Coupe Pompadour
(POMPADOURBECHER)

Ingredients: 1 lb. (500 g.) fruit (pears, pineapples, stoned cherries, strawberries, bananas, etc.), 8 fl. oz. ($\frac{1}{4}$ l.) white wine, 4 eggs, 1 oz. (30 g.) sugar, 1$\frac{3}{4}$ tsp. potato flour, 1 oz. (30 g.) blanched and shredded almonds, $\frac{1}{4}$ pt. ($\frac{1}{8}$ l.) double cream, grated chocolate or cocoa powder.

Prepare the fruit and cut small where necessary. Mix and put in tall serving glasses. Beat the sugar, eggs, wine and potato flour together and cook over a gentle heat, stirring constantly until thick. Add the almonds and pour over the fruit. Top with whipped cream and garnish with chocolate or cocoa powder and a cherry or pineapple piece. Serve at once.

Light Supper Dishes with Fruit

Cold dishes with eggs, cream cheese and fruit are particularly suitable for supper on warm summer evenings as they do not put a burden on the digestive system. Try serving muesli, pineapple on toast, stuffed apples or a fruit mould. Add cream to curd cheese, combine with fruit in season, and a delicious dessert is ready in a matter of minutes.

Buttermilk Cup
(BUTTERMILCH-KALTSCHALE)

Ingredients: 1¼ pt. (¾ l.) buttermilk, 1–2 egg yolks, 1 pkt. (1½ tbsp.) vanilla sugar, 2 oz. (50–70 g.) sugar, 8 oz. (250 g.) strawberries, 1–2 bananas.

Beat the yolks, vanilla sugar and sugar with the buttermilk. Prepare, wash and drain the fruit and carefully combine with the milk. Serve chilled.

Any other soft fruit may be used for this cup and cream may be added.

Raspberry Cup
(HIMBEER-KALTSCHALE)

Ingredients: 1 lb. (500 g.) raspberries, ½ stick cinnamon, 1 oz. (25 g.) potato flour, 1 pkt. (1½ tbsp.) vanilla sugar, sugar.

Prepare the raspberries. Cook half in a pan with a scant ¼ pint (⅛ litre) water and cinnamon. When soft rub through a sieve, add the potato flour to the resulting juice and boil gently until thick. Take from the stove, flavour with sugar and vanilla sugar and leave to cool. Add the remaining raspberries and chill in the refrigerator. Serve with a garnish of meringue or with semolina dumplings.

Other soft fruits may be used similarly.

Fruit Soup Nofretete
(OBSTSUPPE NOFRETETE)

Ingredients: 1½–1¾ lb. (750 g.) fruit (cherries, gooseberries, red-currants, raspberries, apricots or peaches), piece of lemon rind, 1 stick cinnamon, 2–3 tsp. potato flour, 3 oz. (80–100 g.) sugar.

Prepare, wash and stone the fruit. Place all the fruit except the raspberries in a pan with 2½ pints (1½ litres) water, the sugar, lemon rind and cinnamon. Bring to the boil and cook until the fruit is tender. Add the raspberries just before the end of cooking time. Mix the potato flour with a little water, add to the soup to thicken it and boil up once more. Serve chilled, after removing the lemon rind and cinnamon.

Morello Cherries with Yogurt
(SAUERKIRSCHEN MIT JOGHURT)

Ingredients: 1 lb. (500 g.) morello cherries, sugar, ¼–½ pt. (⅛–¼ l.) yogurt, or 1–1¼ pt. (½–¾ l.) sour milk.

Stone the cherries and cook with sugar over a low heat. (Do not add water). When cool, mix the compote with yogurt or sour milk.

Serve with bread and butter as a supper dish.

Copenhagen Strawberries
(KOPENHAGENER ERDBEERSPEISE)

Ingredients: 1½ lb. (750 g.) strawberries, 1 lb. (500 g.) curd cheese, condensed milk, sugar.

Cream the curd cheese with condensed milk and sugar. Wash

and chop the strawberries and combine with the cheese. Serve chilled.

For special occasions fold in whipped cream.

Curd Cheese with Berries
(QUARK-KALTSCHALE)

Ingredients: 1 lb. (500 g.) curd cheese, 2 eggs, pinch of salt, 3½–5 tbsp. sugar, ½ pt. (¼ l.) cream or condensed milk, rum essence, 1 lb. (500 g.) soft fruit (strawberries, raspberries, etc.).

Cream the curd cheese with the egg yolks, salt, sugar and cream or condensed milk. Add rum essence. Prepare the fruit, sieve if preferred, or leave whole and combine with the cheese mixture. Beat the egg whites stiffly, fold in and serve at once.

Curd Cheese with Fruit
(QUARK-PHANTASIE)

Ingredients: 1 lb. (500 g.) curd cheese, 2 eggs, 3½–5 tbsp. sugar, grated rind of ½ lemon, 2 apples, 2 oranges, 2 large peaches (fresh or tinned) or 4 apricots, 3 tbsp. chopped nuts.

Cream the cheese with the egg yolks and sugar. Prepare and chop the fruit (putting some aside for garnish) and add to the cheese mixture. Beat the egg whites stiffly and fold in, together with the grated lemon rind. Sprinkle with the nuts, garnish with fruit, and serve at once. The beaten whites are optional.

Flensburg Beer Soup
(FLENSBURGER BIERSUPPE)

Ingredients: 2 oz. (50–60 g.) breadcrumbs, piece of butter sugar, 2 oz. (50 g.) raisins, 1 egg yolk, 1¼ pt. (¾ l.) stout or light ale.

Lightly fry the breadcrumbs with a little sugar in butter and put into a soup tureen. Soak the raisins in hot water, then add to the breadcrumbs. Beat the yolk with a little water or cold beer in a pan, add the rest of the beer and beat over a low heat until the liquid rises. On no account must the beer be allowed to boil. Pour into the tureen and serve at once.

Budapest Rhubarb Cheese
(BUDAPESTER RHABARBERQUARK)

Ingredients: 1 lb. (500 g.) rhubarb, 1–2 bananas, 3½–5 oz. (100–150 g.) sugar, juice of 1–2 oranges, 5 oz. (150 g.) curd cheese, condensed milk, grated hazelnuts, strawberries or orange slices.

Prepare and chop the rhubarb, peel the bananas and slice thinly. Sprinkle with sugar and orange juice and set aside for half an hour. Meanwhile, beat the curd cheese with the milk and add the hazelnuts. Combine with the fruit and serve with a garnish of strawberries or orange slices.

Stuffed Peaches
(GEFÜLLTE PFIRSICHHÄLFTEN)

Ingredients: 4–6 large peaches, 5–7 oz. (150–200 g.) curd cheese, 1 pkt. (1½ tbsp.) vanilla sugar, sugar.

Wash, halve and stone the peaches. With a small spoon remove some of the flesh and mash this with a fork. Beat the curd cheese with vanilla sugar and sugar to taste and add the fruit pulp. Put the mixture into a forcing bag and pipe a large rosette on each peach half. The peaches can be sandwiched together or arranged separately on a dish. Serve with bread and butter.

Instead of the cheese mixture the peaches could also be filled with vanilla or chocolate ice cream and topped with chocolate sauce. (For this, melt 2 oz. [50 g.] plain chocolate and mix in 1 oz. [25 g.] melted butter.)

Honeyed Pears
(HONIG-BIRNEN)

Ingredients: 3–4 pears, sugar, juice of 2 lemons, 5 tsp. honey, 5 tsp. brandy, 7 fl. oz. (⅕ l.) yogurt.

Peel, halve and core the pears and simmer in water until tender. Leave to cool. Combine the honey, lemon juice and brandy and pour over the fruit. Top with beaten yogurt and serve.

Pears with Cheese
(KÄSE-BIRNEN)

Ingredients: 4 large juicy pears, juice of one lemon, 2 cloves,
2 portions Gervais cheese, 1–1½ oz. (30–40 g.)
butter, 1½ tbsp. chopped chives, paprika.

Peel, halve and core the pears and cook with the lemon juice
and cloves in a little water until tender. Drain on a sieve. Mix
the cheese with the butter and chives and pile a spoonful of the
mixture on top of each pear. Sprinkle with paprika. Serve on a
bed of lettuce leaves or surrounded by watercress, with toast,
rye bread or pumpernickel.

Scrambled Eggs with Oranges
(EIERSPEISE MIT ORANGEN)

Ingredients: 6–7 eggs, 1–2 oranges, pinch of salt, pinch of
ground ginger, butter.

Peel and chop the oranges. Beat the eggs, add the oranges,
salt and ginger. Melt butter in a pan and add the egg mixture.
Cook as for scrambled eggs until all the liquid has disappeared.
Should there be too much orange juice, add a few breadcrumbs
to absorb the surplus. Serve on a dish surrounded by a green
salad.

Roman Cucumber Boats
(RÖMISCHE GURKENSCHIFFCHEN MIT OBST GEFÜLLT)

Ingredients: 2 short thick green cucumbers, 1 large or 2 small
oranges, 2 apples, ½ small celeriac or 1 stick
celery, mayonnaise, condensed milk, lemon juice,
5 tbsp. shredded hazelnuts.

Peel the cucumbers, halve lengthwise and hollow out a little
to form boats. Peel and chop the oranges; peel, core and dice
the apples; shred the celeriac. Mix and sprinkle with lemon
juice and use for dressing the salad. Fill the cucumber boats
with the mixture and sprinkle with hazelnuts.

Hula Dish
(HULA-TELLER)

Ingredients: 1 thick slice of ham (round for preference) per person, same number of pineapple rings, pineapple syrup, juice of 2 oranges, cranberry compote, 1 small glass brandy, butter.

Place the ham slices in a buttered heatproof dish with a ring of pineapples on each. Flavour the cranberry compote with brandy and top each slice with a spoonful. Pour over a cupful of pineapple syrup and the orange juice and place in a fairly hot oven for 5 minutes. Serve with toast.

Serve on a large dish as an accompaniment to cold meats.

Brussels Tomatoes
(BRÜSSELER TOMATENPLATTE)

Ingredients: 1½ lb. (500–750 g.) tomatoes, salt, pepper, 4–6 fresh or tinned peaches, ground ginger, vinegar or lemon juice, condensed milk, lettuce leaves.

Wash and slice the tomatoes, but not too thinly. Arrange on lettuce leaves. Blanch and mash the peaches with a fork and flavour with a pinch of ginger and vinegar or lemon juice. Add enough condensed milk to give the mixture a creamy consistency. Place a spoonful of the mixture on each of the tomato slices and garnish with a small piece of tomato. Serve with curd cheese and rye bread.

Princess Pears à la Madame
(PRINÀESSBIRNENE À LA MADAME)

Ingredients: 2–4 juicy pears, 5–7 oz. (150–200 g.) crab meat, 1 banana, 1 orange, 4 oz. (125 g.) mayonnaise, 1½ tbsp. tomato ketchup, juice of ½ lemon, pinch of paprika, lettuce leaves.

Halve the pears, remove the cores and a little of the flesh. Combine the seasonings with the mayonnaise. Stir in the crab meat and peeled and sliced orange and banana. Fill the pear halves with the mixture and serve on lettuce leaves.

Fried Eggs with Pineapple
(OCHSENAUGEN AUF ANANASSCHEIBEN)

Ingredients: 1 egg and 1 pineapple ring per person, butter, mayonnaise, condensed milk, lemon juice, tomato ketchup, pineapple syrup.

Fry the eggs and pineapple rings separately in butter. Thin the mayonnaise with condensed milk and flavour with lemon juice, pineapple syrup and ketchup. Place the eggs on the pineapple rings and mask with the mayonnaise.

A thick cheese or tomato sauce may be substituted for the mayonnaise.

Pineapple Toast Bali
(ANANASTOAST BALI)

Ingredients per person: 1 Dutch breakfast rusk, 1 slice ham, 1 pineapple ring, 1 slice cheese, 1 egg, butter, paprika.

Butter the rusks, place a piece of ham the same size as the rusk on it, top with a pineapple ring and finally with the cheese. Put on a baking sheet and place in a medium oven until the cheese begins to melt. Meanwhile, separate the eggs and fry the yolks carefully in butter. Beat the whites stiffly and form a nest on top of the cheese. Return to the oven for the whites to colour and set. Finally, place the fried yolks in the nests, dust with paprika and serve.

Banana Bread Florian
(BANANEN-BROTE FLORIAN)

Ingredients: 2 bananas, $2\frac{1}{2}$ oz. (60–80 g.) butter, 1 tbsp. curry powder, juice of 1 lemon, 4 slices bread.

Cream the butter with curry powder and spread the bread slices with it. Place the sliced bananas on the bread, sprinkle with lemon juice and bake in a fairly hot oven for 5–10 minutes.

Apple Slices Volendam
(VOLENDAMER APFELSCHNITTE)

Ingredients: 4 slices Continental rye bread, butter, 2 apples, 4 slices cheese, paprika.

Peel the apples, core and slice very thinly. Place a few rings on the thickly buttered bread. Top with a slice of cheese and bake in the oven or grill. Sprinkle with paprika.

Minced Herring
(HÄCKERLE)

Ingredients: 2–3 herring fillets, 5 oz. (150 g.) fat bacon, 1–2 onions, 1 large apple.

Peel and core the apple. Mince all the ingredients, mix well and shape into a loaf on a serving dish. Serve with boiled potatoes or use as a sandwich spread.

California Grill
(KALIFORNIA GRILLADE)

Ingredients: 4 pairs frankfurters, 8 pineapple rings.

Slice the frankfurters and dice the pineapple. Put on skewers and grill. Serve with bread, butter and olives.

Fried Sausage with Apples
(SCHWARZER MAGISTER)

Ingredients: 14 oz. (400 g.) Continental boiling sausage, fat, 2 large apples, 1 onion.

Slice the sausage and fry in fat. Peel, core and chop the apples and cook in a little water until tender. Drain, mix with the sausage, reheat and serve with a garnish of fried onions.

This quickly prepared dish comes from France.

Hamburg Noodle Pie
(HAMBURGER NUDELPASTETE)

Ingredients: 4–5 apples, 8½ tbsp. sugar, 3½ oz. (100 g.) noodles, salt, grated rind of ½ lemon, 1 oz. (30 g.) blanched and shredded almonds, 1 egg yolk.

For the short-crust pastry: 7 oz. (200 g.) flour, 3½ oz. (100 g.) margarine, pinch of salt, 1 egg, ½ oz. (15 g.) sugar.

146

Make up the pastry and line a fairly deep pie dish with three-quarters of it. Boil the noodles in salt water (1 teaspoon salt per 2 pints [1⅛ litres] water) until tender. Peel, core and chop the apples, mix with the noodles, add the sugar, grated lemon rind and almonds and fill the pastry case with the mixture. Roll out the remaining pastry and cover the dish. Brush with beaten egg yolk and bake in a moderate oven for 30–40 minutes.

Seville Salad
(SALAT SEVILLA)

Ingredients: 1 red and 2 green peppers, 3 oranges, 8 oz. (250 g.) black grapes, brandy, 1 onion, 2½ tbsp. olive oil, 2½–5 tsp. vinegar, salt, paprika.

Cut the peppers near the stalk, remove seeds and inner ribs, wash and cut into thin strips. Make a dressing from 3 parts oil to 1 part vinegar, and salt, and leave the peppers to marinate in it for several hours. Wash the grapes, sprinkle with brandy and arrange in the middle of a serving dish. Peel the oranges, remove the pith and slice thinly or chop. Arrange the oranges round the grapes, garnish with onion rings and sprinkle with paprika. Just before serving add the peppers. Serve with scrambled eggs and bread and butter.

Creamed Peach Salad
(PFIRSICHSALAT MIT QUARKCREME)

Ingredients: 4 peaches, 8 oz. (250 g.) curd cheese, condensed milk, juice of 1 lemon, sugar, 1¼ oz. (30–40 g.) shredded hazelnuts or chopped walnuts, lettuce leaves, salt, French mustard, vinegar, oil.

Skin and halve the peaches, remove the stones. Cream the cheese with the milk and flavour with lemon juice. Sweeten to taste. Top the peach halves with the mixture and sprinkle with the nuts. Make a dressing with oil, vinegar, salt and mustard and pour over the lettuce leaves. Arrange the peaches on the lettuce. Serve with rye bread or pumpernickel.

The curd cheese can be flavoured with salt and tomato ketchup instead of sugar and lemon juice.

Grape Salad
(TRAUBEN-SALAT)

Ingredients: 2–2¼ lb. (1 kg.) black grapes, 1 banana, sugar, 1 glass brandy, 1 oz. (30 g.) walnuts, 1 orange.

Wash the grapes, peel and slice the bananas and place in a bowl. Add sugar, brandy and the walnuts. Peel the orange, divide into quarters and arrange on the salad. If the grapes are large they may be halved. This will increase the juiciness of the salad.

Italian Melon Salad
(ITALIENISCHER MELONENSALAT)

Ingredients: ½ melon, 3–4 tomatoes or 1–2 green peppers, pinch of salt, ¾ tsp. brandy, 3 tbsp. mayonnaise, 3 tbsp. tomato ketchup, 3 tbsp. sour cream, lettuce leaves.

Scoop out the flesh of the melon with a silver spoon and cut up. Chop the tomatoes, or shred the peppers after removing the seeds. Sprinkle with salt and brandy. Mix the mayonnaise with ketchup and sour cream and pour over the salad. Arrange on lettuce leaves.

Serve in the ancient Roman tradition with cheese and bread and butter.

Rice Salad with Cheese Sauce
(REISSALAT MIT QUARKSAUCE)

Ingredients: 1 apple, 1 orange, 1 slice of melon, pineapple pieces or 2 rings, 1 peach, a little boiled rice, 3½ oz. (100 g.) curd cheese, 2½–5 tsp. milk, grated rind of 1 lemon, juice of 1 orange.

Cut all the fruit into neat pieces and mix with the rice. Cream the cheese with the milk, flavour with grated lemon rind and orange juice and combine with the fruit.

Salad Paola
(SALAT PAOLA)

Ingredients: 3 heads chicory, pineapple pieces or 2–3 rings, 1 carrot, 2–3 tbsp. curd cheese, 4 fl. oz. ($\frac{1}{10}$ l.) yogurt, juice of $1\frac{1}{2}$ lemons, salt.

Trim the chicory and remove any discoloured leaves. Slice thinly and soak in lukewarm water for 1–2 hours. Shred the pineapple and carrot, drain the chicory slices. Beat the yogurt with the curd cheese, flavour with lemon juice and salt and combine with the salad ingredients. Serve with fried potatoes.

Wuerzburg Salad
(WÜRZBURGER SALAT)

Ingredients: 2–3 apples, 1 orange, 8 oz. (250 g.) curd cheese, cream, parsley, cos lettuce, $\frac{1}{2}$ grapefruit, $\frac{1}{2}$ pt. ($\frac{1}{4}$ l.) yogurt, $2\frac{1}{2}$ tsp. salad oil, pinch of sugar.

Peel, core and slice the apples, peel and chop the orange. Add cream and chopped parsley to the curd cheese. Place it in the centre of an oval dish and surround with apple slices and pieces of orange. Wash and dry the lettuce, mix with chopped grapefruit and put round the edges of the dish. Make a dressing from the yogurt, oil and sugar and pour over the salad.

It tastes delicious and is rich in vitamins.

Apples with Meat Salad
(GEFÜLLTE GRAFENSTEINER)

Ingredients: 4 large apples, juice of $1\frac{1}{2}$ lemons, $1–1\frac{1}{2}$ cooked pork chops, $1–1\frac{1}{2}$ tomatoes, 1 sour gherkin, 1 hard-boiled egg, mayonnaise, tomato ketchup, 4 olives.

Peel and core the apples and scoop out as much of the flesh as possible without breaking them. Sprinkle with lemon juice. Chop the meat, tomatoes, gherkin and egg finely. Flavour mayonnaise with ketchup, combine the other ingredients with it and fill the apples with the mixture. Garnish each with an olive.

The quantitites will vary according to size and capacity of the apples.

Beef Salad with Apples

(FLEISCHSALAT MIT ÄPFELN)

Ingredients: ¾ lb. (375 g.) cooked lean beef, 3 juicy apples, juice of 1 lemon, 2 sweet-and-sour gherkins, 1 onion, 4 oz. (125 g.) mayonnaise, condensed milk, French mustard, tomato ketchup.

Dice the meat. Peel, core and slice the apples and sprinkle with lemon juice. Chop the gherkins and onion finely. Dilute the mayonnaise with milk and season with ketchup and mustard. Mix well together.

Instead of mayonnaise an ordinary dressing of oil, vinegar, salt and pepper may be used.

Husum Apples

(HUSUMER ÄPFEL)

Ingredients: 2–3 large juicy apples, 5–7 oz. (150–200 g.) crab meat, ½ oz. (15 g.) fat, ½ oz. (15 g.) flour, scant ½ pt. (¼ l.) milk and condensed milk mixed, pinch of salt, 2 oz. (50 g.) Gruyère cheese, 1–1½ tsp. tomato ketchup, butter, 1 tomato, 1 hard-boiled egg, lettuce leaves.

Halve the apples and scoop out the centres. Make a roux with the fat and flour, add the milk and simmer until the sauce thickens. Add the cheese and cook until melted. Mix in the crab meat and tomato ketchup. Stuff the apples with the mixture, place in a buttered heatproof dish and bake in a moderate oven for 20–30 minutes. Garnish with a slice of tomato and hard-boiled egg and serve surrounded by lettuce leaves.

Floret Salad

(FLORETT-SALAT)

Ingredients: 3 juicy apples, 3 oranges, lemon juice, 2 oz. (50 g.) walnuts, 5 oz. (150 g.) cream cheese, paprika, parsley.

Core the apples. Slice the apples and oranges and arrange overlapping on a serving dish. Sprinkle the apple slices with lemon juice to prevent discoloration. Chop the walnuts and scatter over the fruit. Season the cheese with paprika and chopped parsley and garnish the salad with spoonfuls of the cheese mixture.

Apple Salad Beatrix
(APFELSALAT NACH BEATRIX)

Ingredients: 4 large apples, 1–2 onions, 2 Frankfurter sausages, lemon juice or vinegar, olive oil, salt, pepper.

Peel, core and dice the apples. Chop the onions finely. Make a dressing with the lemon juice or vinegar, oil, salt and pepper and combine. Slice the sausages thinly and add to the salad. Leave for an hour or so before serving.

Mayonnaise may be used instead of the salad dressing. Alternatively, mix the diced apple with chopped walnuts and dress with lemon-flavoured mayonnaise.

Syrian Salad
(SYRISCHER SALAT)

Ingredients: 3 bananas, 3½ oz. (100 g.) cooked rice, 3½ oz. (100 g.) crab meat, 3½ tbsp. olive oil, juice of ½ lemon, pinch of curry powder, Worcestershire sauce.

Peel and slice the bananas and mix with the rice and crab meat. Make a dressing with the oil, lemon juice and curry powder, beat it well with a fork, add a dash of Worcestershire sauce and combine the salad.

Fish Salad Marseilles
(MARSEILLER FISCHSALAT)

Ingredients: 1 lb. (500 g.) cooked potatoes, 2 apples, 1 small, cooked celeriac or 2 sticks celery, 4 oz. (125 g.) each of cooked peas, runner beans and carrots, 3 herring fillets, 7 oz. (200 g.) mayonnaise, salt, pepper, tomato ketchup, lemon juice.

Peel the potatoes and the apples. Slice the potatoes and the herrings. Dice the apples, celeriac or celery and carrots. Fold

the seasonings into the mayonnaise and combine all the salad
ingredients.

Senator's Salad
(SENATOREN-SALAT)

Ingredients: 5–6 cooked potatoes, 1 small (2 oz. [50 g.]) tin
garden peas, 1–2 pairs Vienna sausages or 5 oz.
(150 g.) salami, 1–2 pineapple rings, $4\frac{1}{2}$ oz. (125 g.)
mayonnaise, $2\frac{1}{2}$–5 tsp. condensed milk, horseradish, 1 hard-boiled egg.

Peel and dice the potatoes; slice the sausage and pineapple.
Dilute the mayonnaise with the milk and flavour with horse-
radish. Add the peas and mix all the ingredients together.
Arrange on a serving dish and garnish with chopped egg.

Herring Salad à la Maison
(HERINGSALAT NACH ART DES HAUSES)

Ingredients: 2–$2\frac{1}{4}$ lb. (1 kg.) cooked potatoes, 2 fresh or salted
herring fillets, 1–2 onions, 1–2 apples, $3\frac{1}{2}$ tbsp.
oil, $1\frac{3}{4}$ tbsp. vinegar, pepper, paprika, 2 tbsp.
beef stock, 1 hard-boiled egg, capers.

If salted herrings are used they must be soaked for 24 hours
beforehand, changing the water frequently. Chop the onions,
herrings and peeled apples. Peel and slice the potatoes. Make
a dressing from the oil, vinegar and stock, season with paprika
and pepper and toss with the salad. Serve with a garnish of
chopped egg and capers.

Rice Pudding with Strawberry Sauce
(STETTENER REISBERG MIT ERDBEERMARK)

Ingredients: 8 oz. (250 g.) pudding rice, $\frac{3}{4}$ pt. ($\frac{1}{2}$ l.) milk, 3 oz.
(80–100 g.) sugar, 1 pkt. ($1\frac{1}{2}$ tbsp.) vanilla sugar,
1 lb. (500 g.) strawberries, double cream.

Cook the rice in plenty of fast-boiling water for 10 minutes.
Drain, add the milk and cook until the rice is tender. Sweeten
with 3–5 tablespoons sugar. Rinse a dish with cold water, put
the rice in, let it cool and then chill in the refrigerator for

several hours. Rub the strawberries through a sieve and sweeten with sugar and vanilla sugar. Turn the rice out on a serving dish, pour the sauce over and top with whipped cream if desired.

Rum or brandy may be added to the strawberry sauce.

Salzburg Rice Schmarren
(SALZBURGER REISSCHMARREN)

Ingredients: 8 oz. (250 g.) pudding rice, pinch of salt, milk, 3 eggs, 1 oz. (30 g.) butter, fat, sugar and cinnamon.

Wash the rice well and cook with milk and the salt until quite soft. Stir in the beaten eggs and a little butter. Heat fat in a pan and fry part of the mixture until golden, brushing it with more butter if it should get too dry. Cut off portions of the schmarren with a spoon and turn until done all over. Continue until all the mixture is used up. Arrange in a serving dish and sprinkle with sugar and cinnamon. Serve with compote.

Black Peter
(SCHWARZER PETER)

Ingredients: 1 lb. (500 g.) curd cheese, ½–¾ pt. (⅜ l.) milk, 1–1½ oz. (30–40 g.) sugar, 1 lb. (500 g.) bilberries, sugar and cinnamon.

Sieve the curd cheese, add the milk and sugar and beat well. Wash and drain the bilberries and stir them in just before serving. Serve sugar and cinnamon separately.

Soft fruits other than bilberries, or chopped pineapple or peaches can be used in the same way.

Bread Pudding Melanie
(WECKAUFLAUF MELANIE)

Ingredients: 7–8 stale rolls, 1–1¼ pt. (½–¾ l.) milk, 2 eggs, 1 pkt. (1½ tbsp.) vanilla sugar, 5 tbsp. sugar, 1 oz. (30 g.) blanched and shredded almonds, 1½ lb. (500–750 g.) fruit (cherries, gooseberries, plums, chopped apples), butter.

Slice the rolls. Put a layer in a buttered heatproof dish, top with a layer of fruit and continue in this way until all the fruit and bread is used up. Scatter almonds between the layers and finish with a layer of bread. Beat the milk with the eggs, flavour with sugar and vanilla sugar and pour over the pudding. Dot with butter and bake in a moderate oven for 20–30 minutes.

The fruit may be omitted and the pudding served with compote instead. In this case more milk should be used to keep the pudding moist.

Redcurrant Pudding
(JOHANNISBEERPUDDING)

Ingredients: ¾–1 lb. (375–500 g.) redcurrants, ¾ pt. (½ l.) milk, 1 pkt. (2 tbsp.) custard powder, 7½ tbsp. sugar, 4–8 oz. (125–250 g.) curd cheese.

Prepare and wash the fruit and sprinkle with sugar. Make up the custard and sweeten. Mix with the curd cheese, then add the redcurrants. Serve cold and decorate with a few redcurrants.

All other kinds of soft fruit are also suitable for this pudding.

Baked Rhubarb
(ÜBERBACKENER RHABARBER)

Ingredients: 1 lb. (500 g.) rhubarb, 5 oz. (150 g.) sugar, rind of ½ lemon, butter, 2 oz. (50 g.) ground hazelnuts, 3 egg whites, 3½ oz. (100 g.) icing sugar.

Prepare the rhubarb, cut into small pieces and cook in as little water as possible until it forms a thick compote. Flavour with sugar and lemon rind. Put the fruit into a buttered heatproof dish and strew with the hazelnuts. Stiffly beat the whites, fold in the icing sugar, put the mixture in a forcing bag and pipe rosettes all over the top. Place the dish in a cool oven for 5–10 minutes.

Rhubarb Pie
(WARME RHABARBERPASTETE)

Ingredients: 1 lb. (500 g.) rhubarb, 8 oz. (250 g.) sugar, cinnamon, grated lemon rind, egg yolk, butter.

For the pastry: 10 oz. (300 g.) flour, 2¾ oz. (80 g.) margarine, 4¼ oz. (125 g.) sugar, grated rind of ½ lemon, 1 egg, 1 tsp. baking powder, 1¾ tbsp. milk.

Make up the pastry. Roll out and line a buttered pie dish with the dough. Wash and cut up the rhubarb, mix it with the sugar, cinnamon and a little grated lemon rind and fill the pastry case with the mixture. Cut the remaining dough into strips and form a lattice on top of the fruit. Brush this with beaten egg yolk and bake the pie in a cool oven for 45–60 minutes. Serve with cream or cold milk.

If preferred, the lattice pattern may be glazed with thin sugar icing.

Graz Lemon Rice Ring
(GRAZER ZITRONENSPEISE IM RING)

Ingredients: ¾ lb. (375 g.) pudding rice, sugar, ¼ pt. (⅛ l.) white wine, 5 tsp. lemon juice, 1 egg yolk, 1 pkt. (1½ tbsp.) vanilla sugar, butter, 8 oz. (250 g.) tinned or fresh soft fruit, sugar, rum or brandy.

Wash the rice, bring to the boil in plenty of water, drain and separate the grains with cold water. Repeat the process but cook for 10–15 minutes this time. Now pour the wine over the rice, add the sugar and cook over a low heat until all the wine has been absorbed and the rice is tender. Some more wine may have to be added. Stir in the beaten yolk, vanilla sugar and lemon juice, then turn the rice into a well buttered ring mould. Chill. When firm, turn the mixture on to a dish. Rub the fruit through a sieve, sweeten, and flavour with rum or brandy if desired. Arrange the purée on the rice and garnish with whole berries or banana slices.

Orange juice may be used similarly to lemon.

Prague Rice Pudding with Plums
(PRAGER REISAUFLAUF MIT PFLAUMEN)

Ingredients: 7 oz. (200 g.) pudding rice, scant ½ pt. (¼ l.) milk, 3 oz. (80 g.) sugar, pinch of salt, 1½–1¾ lb. (750 g.) plums, 2–3 egg whites, pinch of baking powder, 3½ oz. (100 g.) icing sugar, 4 oz. (100–120 g.) ground almonds.

Bring the rice to the boil in plenty of water, drain, bring to the boil again in the milk and an equal amount of water and cook until tender but not mushy. Drain, add sugar and salt, then place half the rice in a buttered heatproof dish. Wash and stone the plums, put over the rice in the dish and top with the remaining rice. Bake in a moderate oven for about 20 minutes. In the meantime, beat the egg whites stiffly with the baking powder and fold in the icing sugar and almonds. Arrange the mixture over the pudding and return to the oven for a further 5–10 minutes.

Quinces with Rice
(WARME QUITTENSPEISE MIT REIS)

Ingredients: 1 lb. (500 g.) quinces, 7 oz. (200 g.) sugar, 1 stick cinnamon, rind of 1 lemon, 9 oz. (250 g.) pudding rice, pinch of salt, butter, 3 egg whites, 3½ oz. (100 g.) icing sugar.

Peel, core and slice the quinces. Simmer the fruit with sugar, cinnamon and lemon rind in a little water until tender. Wash the rice, bring to the boil, drain, add cold salted water and cook for 10 minutes. Drain on a sieve. Lift the quince slices out of the syrup, remove the cinnamon and lemon rind and cook the rice in the fruit syrup until tender. Butter a heatproof dish and fill it with alternate layers of fruit and rice. Beat the egg whites stiffly, fold in the icing sugar and pipe a lattice pattern on top. Bake in a moderate oven for 10–15 minutes until the meringue turns golden.

Bavarian Cheese Pudding
(QUARKAUFLAUF OBERBAYRISCH)

Ingredients: 5 oz. (150 g.) sugar, 3–4 eggs, 2½ oz . (80 g.) margarine, 1¾ oz. (50 g.) semolina, 1 lb. (500 g.) curd cheese, pinch of salt, grated rind of 1 lemon, 1 lb. (500 g.) fresh or bottled fruit (cherries, apricots or apples), butter, icing sugar.

Cream the sugar with the margarine and egg yolks, add the curd cheese, semolina, salt and grated lemon rind, and finally the stiffly beaten egg whites. Stone the cherries or, if using apricots or apples, chop these or slice thinly. Fill a buttered heatproof dish with alternating layers of fruit and cheese mixture and bake for 30–45 minutes at a moderate temperature. Sprinkle with icing sugar and serve with a fruit, vanilla or chocolate sauce.

Red Fruit Mould
(ROTER WACKELPETER)

Ingredients: 1 lb. (500 g.) redcurrants, 8 oz. (250 g.) gooseberries, 8 oz. (250 g.) raspberries, 5 oz. (130–150 g.) potato flour, 6½ oz. (180–200 g.) sugar, 1 oz. (30 g.) blanched and chopped almonds or grated hazelnuts.

Prepare the fruit, cook in 2¼ pints (1¼ litres) water, then sieve. Mix the potato flour with a little water until quite smooth and thicken the fruit juice (of which there should be about 2½ pints [1½ litres]) over a low heat, stirring constantly. Add the sugar and continue cooking. Rinse a mould or glass dish with cold water, sprinkle with almonds or hazelnuts and pour in the fruit mixture. Chill. Unmould when quite firm and serve with vanilla custard.

Alternatively, stir 8 oz. (250 g.) curd cheese into the hot fruit mixture and leave to set.

Rice Medals with Glazed Pears
(REISTALER MIT GLASIERTEN BIRNEN)

Ingredients: 8 oz. (250 g.) rice, ¾ pt. (½ l.) milk, 2–3 tbsp. sugar, grated rind of 1 lemon, 3–4 pears, ½ stick cinnamon, cranberry compote or redcurrant jelly, brandy.

Wash the rice and cook with the milk and sugar until quite soft. Brush a baking tray with oil. When the rice is cool, spread on the tray in a layer about ½ inch thick. Leave until firm. In the meantime peel, core and slice the pears, cook with cinnamon and sugar in a little water until tender, drain and leave to cool. Dip the rim of a cup in water and cut out rice medals. Place them on a dish and arrange the pear slices on top. Warm the jelly or compote, dilute with a little water or brandy and brush the fruit with it.

Grape Pudding Ariane
(TRAUBENPUDDING ARIANE)

Ingredients: 6 rolls, milk, 2–3 eggs, 3½ oz. (100 g.) butter or margarine, 5½ oz. (150 g.) sugar, 2 oz. (60 g.) ground almonds or hazelnuts, cinnamon, grated rind of 1 lemon, 3¼ lb. (1½ kg.) grapes.

Remove the crusts from the rolls and soak the soft parts in a little warm milk. Squeeze out the surplus liquid. Cream the butter or margarine with the sugar and egg yolks, add flavourings and the shredded rolls. Wash the grapes, add to the mixture, then fold in the stiffly beaten egg whites. Place the mixture in a buttered pudding basin and steam for ¾ hour. Serve with wine or chocolate sauce or vanilla custard.

Baked Pears
(BIRNEN IM TEIG)

Ingredients: 1½–1¾ oz. (40–50 g.) potato flou r, 1¾ pt. (1 l.) milk, 5 eggs, pinch of salt, 5–7 tbsp. sugar, grated rind of ½ lemon, 3–4 pears, butter.

Mix the potato flour with a little of the milk to a smooth paste. Add to the remaining milk in a pan and bring slowly to the boil, stirring constantly. Cook for a short time but do not allow the milk to get too thick. Put aside to cool. Beat the egg yolks with the sugar, salt and grated lemon rind and add to the milk. Finally, fold in the stiffly beaten egg whites. Peel, core and slice the pears and cook for a short time in a very little sweetened water until softened slightly. Place the pears in a buttered heatproof dish, top with the milk mixture and bake in a moderate oven for a ½ hour. Serve with lemon sauce or more pear compote.

Apple Mosaic

(APFELMOSAIK)

Ingredients: 5–6 cooking apples, juice of 1 lemon, rind of
$\frac{1}{2}$ orange, $8\frac{1}{2}$ tbsp. sugar, $\frac{1}{2}$ tsp. cinnamon, 3 oz.
(90 g.) flour, 2 eggs, milk, butter.

Peel, core and quarter the apples. Put them into a buttered
heatproof dish and pour the lemon juice over. Sprinkle with
finely chopped orange rind and a little sugar and the cinnamon.
Make a fairly thick batter from the eggs and flour, sugar and
milk, and distribute this over the apples. Bake in a moderate
oven for approximately 40 minutes.

Fruit Dishes for Children

Children are naturally attracted to fruit and it is not difficult to devise fruit dishes which are especially suitable for inclusion in children's diets all the year round. Even a simple dish of fresh fruit, sprinkled with sugar, topped with cream and served with bread and butter provides all the necessary nutrients. Curd cheese, buttermilk or yogurt are liked by many children, and curd cheese mixed with a little milk and flavoured with chopped mango chutney is popular as a sandwich spread. Most fruit puddings are suitable for the junior diet. Sultanas and raisins should always be soaked in water first to make them more palatable. In pancake batters, sour milk may be used instead of sweet milk, or a mixture of a combination of half milk, half cream or half mineral water may be used. All puddings and flummeries are improved in appearance and flavour by a topping of fruit juice or purée. Blackcurrant juice is particularly rich in vitamin C. The nutritive value of sweet dishes can be increased by using honey as a sweetener instead of sugar.

Rhubarb Pudding Ulrike
(RHABARBERAUFLAUF ULRIKE)

Ingredients: 1 lb. (500 g.) rhubarb, 7–9 oz. (200–250 g.) sugar,
rind of 1 lemon, 1 pkt. rusks, 2½–3 oz. (80 g.)
potato flour, 2–3 eggs, ¾–1 pt. (½ l.) milk or buttermilk, breadcrumbs, butter.

Peel the rhubarb and cook it in its own juice with sugar and
lemon rind over a low heat. Care must be taken at the beginning to prevent its sticking. Remove the lemon rind and place
the rhubarb and rusks in alternate layers in a buttered heatproof dish. Beat the eggs and add sugar, the potato flour and
the milk, a little at first, then the remainder. When quite
smooth, pour over the pudding, sprinkle with breadcrumbs,
dot with butter and bake in a moderate oven for 40–50
minutes.

Rhubarb in Pancake Batter
(RHABARBER IN EIERKUCHENTEIG)

Ingredients: 1 lb. (500 g.) rhubarb, rind of ½ lemon, 5 oz.
(150 g.) sugar, fat, mixed sugar and cinnamon.
For the batter: 4½ oz. (125 g.) flour, pinch of salt, 1 egg, scant
½ pt. (¼ l.) milk.

Skin and chop the rhubarb into small pieces and cook in ½ pint
(¼ litre) water with lemon rind and sugar for 3–4 minutes.
The pieces should remain whole. Drain. Make up a thick
batter, coat the rhubarb pieces and fry in hot fat. Serve sprinkled
with mixed sugar and cinnamon.

Rhubarb with Sago
(RHABARBERGRÜTZE MIT SAGO)

Ingredients: 1½–1¾ lb. (750 g.) rhubarb, juice and grated rind
of 1 lemon, 7–9 oz. (200–250 g.) sugar, 2½ oz.
(75 g.) sago, 2½ tbsp. rum or fruit juice.

Wash the rhubarb and cut into 1 inch long pieces. Place in a
pan with the lemon juice and rind, sugar and 1 pint (½ litre)
water and bring to the boil. Thicken with the sago, take off the
heat and flavour with the rum or fruit juice. Pour into a serv-

ing bowl previously rinsed with water and leave to cool.
Serve with vanilla custard.

Linz Nockerln
(LINZER NOCKERLN)

Ingredients: 9 oz. (250 g.) flour, 2 eggs, ½ oz. (15 g.) yeast,
scant ½ pt. (¼ l.) milk, 1¾ oz. (50 g.) margarine,
1½–2 oz. (40–60 g.) sugar, 1½–1¾ lb. (750 g.)
cherries, fat, breadcrumbs, sugar and cinnamon.

Combine the yeast with a little lukewarm milk, stir into a
smooth paste and leave for 10 minutes. Add the flour, egg
yolks, margarine, sugar, the rest of the milk and finally the
stiffly beaten egg whites. Mix well, cover with a cloth and set
aside. Stone the cherries. When the dough is well risen, cut out
pieces of the mixture with a tablespoon, place 3–4 cherries on
each and form nockerln (oval-shaped dumplings), sealing well
all round. Set aside once more to rise. Fry in deep fat and
serve sprinkled with fried breadcrumbs, sugar and cinnamon.

Alternatively, nockerln can be prepared from choux pastry
and these are equally delicious.

Corinthian Rice Pudding
KÄRNTNER REISAUFLAUF)

Ingredients: 8 oz. (250 g.) pudding rice, pinch of salt, 1¼–1¾ pt.
(¾–1 l.) milk, 7½ tbsp. sugar, juice of 1 orange,
grated rind and juice of 1 lemon, 1½ lb. (750 g.)
cherries, 8 oz. (250 g.) curd cheese, butter.

Wash the rice and bring to the boil in salted water. Drain,
bring to the boil in fresh water and cook for 10 minutes. Drain,
separate the grains with cold water. Cook with the milk over a
low heat until thick. Flavour with orange juice and grated
lemon rind and sweeten with sugar. Wash and stone the
cherries, and add to the creamed curd cheese. Flavour with
lemon juice. Fill a buttered heatproof dish with layers of rice
and cherries, dot with butter and bake for about 30 minutes
in a moderate oven.

Instead of butter the pudding may be topped with stiffly

beaten egg white, just before the end of baking time. Alternatively, this pudding can be made with pineapple pieces and served with cream, in which case the meringue topping should be omitted.

Sour Cherry Pudding
(ROTER SAUERKIRSCHEN PUDDING)

Ingredients: 1 lb. (500 g.) stoned sour cherries, 8 oz. (250 g.) sugar, grated rind of 1 lemon, 4 oz. (125 g.) sago.

Place the cherries in a pan with $1\frac{1}{2}$–$1\frac{3}{4}$ pints (1 litre) water, the sugar and grated lemon rind and cook for 5 minutes. Add the sago and simmer until it softens and becomes transparent. Leave to cool a little, pour into a warmed glass dish, then chill. Serve with custard.

Cherry Pudding Johanne
(KIRSCHENSPEISE JOHANNA)

Ingredients: 1–2 pkt. unsweetened rusks ($10\frac{1}{2}$ oz. [300 g.]), $1\frac{3}{4}$–$2\frac{1}{4}$ lb. (750–1000 g.) cherries, $1\frac{1}{4}$ pt. ($\frac{3}{4}$ l.) milk, 3 oz. (80–100 g.) sugar, 3 eggs, 1 oz. (30 g.) butter, $1\frac{1}{2}$ tbsp. fresh breadcrumbs.

Butter a deep heatproof dish and line the bottom with a layer of rusks. Sprinkle with sugar, add a layer of stoned cherries. Repeat the layers until the dish is three-quarters full. Add the well beaten eggs and the sugar to the milk and pour over the mixture in the dish. Sprinkle the top with breadcrumbs, dot with butter and bake in a moderate oven. Serve with fruit syrup.

Cherry Pudding à la Katrin
(KIRSCHENPUDDING À LA KATRIN)

Ingredients: $1\frac{1}{4}$ lb. (600 g.) black cherries, $3\frac{1}{2}$ oz. (100 g.) margarine, 4 eggs, $3\frac{1}{2}$ oz. (100 g.) sugar, $4\frac{1}{2}$ oz. (125 g.) breadcrumbs, $5\frac{1}{2}$ oz. (150 g.) flour, $\frac{1}{2}$ pkt. ($1\frac{1}{4}$ tsp.) baking powder, pinch of cinnamon, 1 pkt. ($1\frac{1}{2}$ tbsp.) vanilla sugar, juice of $\frac{1}{2}$ lemon or orange, rum essence, 6–7 tbsp. milk, butter.

Wash and stone the cherries. Cream the margarine with the

sugar and beat in the egg yolks. Add three-quarters of the breadcrumbs, the sifted flour and baking powder and then the milk and flavourings. Fold in the stiffly beaten egg whites and the cherries. Butter a large pudding basin (the pudding will rise during cooking), sprinkle with the remaining bread-crumbs, fill with the mixture and steam for 60–70 minutes. Turn out and serve with chocolate or wine sauce, or with sour milk.

Tinned or bottled cherries, or seedless grapes may be used instead of fresh fruit. Drain and use the syrup for soft drinks or fruit sauces.

Coral Pudding
(KORALLEN-AUFLAUF)

Ingredients: 1¾ pt. (1 l.) milk, 9 oz. (250 g.) semolina, knob of butter, 4 oz. (120 g.) sugar, grated lemon rind, 2 eggs, 1¾ lb. (750 g.) black cherries.

For the topping: Knob of butter, 3½ tbsp. sugar, 1½–2 tbps. milk, 1–2 oz. (30–50 g.) chopped hazelnuts.

Cook the semolina in milk until thick. Remove the pan from the stove and stir in the butter, sugar, grated lemon rind and egg yolks. Wash and stone the cherries and add to the semo-lina. Fold in the stiffly beaten egg whites. Pile the mixture into a buttered heatproof dish and bake in a moderate oven for 20–30 minutes. In the meantime, melt butter in a pan, add the sugar and cook, stirring constantly, until the mixture colours. Quickly add the milk and hazelnuts and continue to stir until the caramel topping is ready. Pour on to a plate or wooden board which has been rinsed with cold water. When set, chop the caramel and sprinkle on top of the pudding. Serve hot.

Strawberry Chocolate Flummery
(ERDBEER-SCHOKOLADENFLAMMERI)

Ingredients: 1¼ pt. (¾ l.) milk, 1 oz. (30 g.) cocoa, pinch of salt, 3 oz. (90 g.) semolina, 2 oz. (60 g.) sugar, 1 pkt. (1½ tbsp.) vanilla sugar, 1 egg, 1 oz. (30 g.) ground almonds, ½ tsp. rum essence, 13 oz. (375 g.) strawberries.

Cream the cocoa with a little cold milk, add the rest of the milk, salt and sugar and bring to the boil. Stir in the semolina and simmer for a short time. Remove from the heat, add the egg yolk, rum essence and almonds and beat until the mixture is cool. Fold in the stiffly beaten egg white and some of the strawberries, washed drained and chopped. Chill and serve decorated with strawberries coated with vanilla sugar.

Strawberry Slices Royale
(ERDBEERSCHNITTEN ROYAL)

Ingredients: 5 slices stale bread, ¾–1 pt. (½ l.) milk, 2–3 egg yolks, 1 lb. (500 g.) strawberries, 2 pkt. (3 tbsp.) vanilla sugar, fat, sugar and cinnamon.

Dip the bread slices in milk, then in the beaten yolks. Wash and hull the strawberries, mash with a fork and sweeten with vanilla sugar. Spread the purée on one side of the prepared bread and fry the other side quickly in hot fat. Arrange the slices on a dish and sprinkle with sugar and cinnamon.

Alternatively, dip the bread slices in red wine, sandwich together in pairs with strawberry filling, dip in egg yolk and fry on both sides. This version, however, should be reserved for adults.

Raspberries can be used similarly to strawberries.

Redcurrant Semolina Pudding
(JOHANNISBEER-GRIESS-SPEISE)

Ingredients: 1 lb. (500 g.) bottled or tinned redcurrants, 1½–2¼ oz. (50–60 g.) semolina, grated rind of ½ lemon, sugar.

Drain the redcurrants well on a sieve and make the juice up to ¾–1 pint (½ litre) with water. Add the semolina and grated lemon rind to the liquid and cook slowly, beating or stirring constantly, until thick. Sweeten to taste, add the fruit and turn into a pudding bowl which has been rinsed with water. When cool, turn out and serve with vanilla- or chocolate-flavoured custard.

Blackcurrant Mould
(SCHWARZE GRÜTZE)

Ingredients: 2 lb. (1 kg.) blackcurrants, 5–6 oz. (150–180 g.)
potato flour, 8–10 oz. (250–300 g.) sugar.

Wash and hull the fruit, cook it in 2½ pints (1½ litres) water
until tender and rub through a sieve. Blend the potato flour
with some of the liquid, add it to the rest of the fruit juice and
cook slowly until thick. Add the sugar and bring to the boil
once more. Rinse a bowl with cold water and pour in the fruit
mixture. Chill. Turn out when set and serve with vanilla
custard.

Gooseberry Pudding
(STACHELBEERAUFLAUF, EINFACH)

Ingredients: 5–7 oz. (150–200 g.) biscuit- or breadcrumbs, 1½–
1¾ lb. (750 g.) gooseberries, butter, 3 eggs, 2½–3
oz. (80 g.) sugar, 3½–5 tbsp. flour, grated rind of
½ lemon, vanilla sugar, scant ½ pt. (¼ litre) milk.

Top and tail the washed gooseberries, mix them with the
crumbs and pile the fruit into a buttered heatproof dish. Beat
the egg yolks with the sugar, flour and flavourings, add the
milk and fold in the stiffly beaten egg whites. Distribute the
mixture over the fruit and bake in a moderate oven for about
25–30 minutes.

Apricot Pudding Melanie
(APRIKOSENPUDDING MELANIE)

Ingredients: 4 oz. (100 g.) margarine, 4 oz. (100 g.) sugar, 4 eggs,
4 oz. (100 g.) breadcrumbs, 1 oz. (25 g.) grated
hazelnuts, 5½ oz. (150 g.) flour, 1¾ tsp. baking
powder, 4–5 tbsp. milk, pinch of cocoa powder,
1 pkt. (1½ tbsp.) vanilla sugar, juice of 1 lemon,
1–1¼ lb. (500 g.) stoned apricots, butter.

Cream the margarine with the sugar and beat in the egg yolks.
Add the breadcrumbs, hazelnuts, the sifted flour and baking

167

powder, milk, flavourings, and finally the stiffly beaten egg whites. The apricots should be soft and juicy. If somewhat under-ripe they should first be blanched and then poached in a little water. Drain and cool before adding to the pudding mixture. Turn into a buttered pudding basin which should be large enough to allow for the pudding to rise. Steam for 1 hour. Turn out and serve with fruit syrup. Sprinkle with sugar if desired.

Peaches, plums, cherries and all other stone-fruits can be used with equal success for this pudding. Well drained bottled or tinned fruit will serve out of season, with the advantage of providing ready-made fruit sauce. And few children are likely to refuse an accompanying vanilla custard or chocolate sauce. This is a very filling dish.

Fried Cranberry Slices
(PREISELBEERPAVESEN)

Ingredients: 5–6 slices of bread, ¾–1 pt. (½ l.) milk, 2–3 eggs, breadcrumbs, fat, cranberry compote.

Cut the bread slices into strips about ¾–1 inch wide, place them in a bowl, pour over the lukewarm milk. Lift the strips out, taking care to keep them whole. Turn the strips in beaten egg, coat with breadcrumbs and fry in hot fat on both sides until crisp. Top with cranberries.

Instead of cranberries use stewed sliced pears, or a combination of both.

Black Forest Fruit Mountain
(SCHWARZWÄLDER OBSTBERG)

Ingredients: ¾–1 pt. (½ l.) milk, rind of ½ lemon, 2 oz. (60 g.) semolina, 2–3 oz. (60–80 g.) desiccated coconut, 3½ tbsp. sugar, 1 egg, ¾ lb. (375 g.) bilberries, extra sugar.

Pour the milk into a pan, stir in the semolina, add the lemon rind and bring to the boil. Cook for a minute or two, then add the sugar and coconut. Take off the heat, stir in the beaten egg yolk and finally fold in the stiffly beaten white. Rinse a pudding mould with cold water, pile in the flummery and chill. Turn out on a serving dish and arrange the sugared bilberries on top.

Bilberry Crêpes Liebenzell
(LIEBENZELLER HEIDELBEER-CRÈPES)

Ingredients: 9–10½ oz. (260–300 g.) flour, 2 eggs, salt, ¾–1 pt. (½ l.) milk, fat, 1½ lb. (500–750 g.) bilberries, sugar.

Prepare a fairly thin pancake batter from the flour, eggs, salt and milk. Fry thin pancakes. Prepare, wash and drain the bilberries well. Put a spoonful on each crêpe, roll up, sprinkle with sugar and serve. This quantity makes about 12 crêpes.

Wood Pile [Bread and Butter Pudding]
(SCHEITERHAUFEN)

Ingredients: 5–7 stale rolls or the equivalent in bread, ¾–1 pt. (½ l.) milk, 1½ lb. (500–750 g.) pears, apples or peaches, 4 eggs, 1 tin condensed milk, milk, 3 oz. (90 g.) sugar, butter.

Slice the rolls and soak briefly in lukewarm milk, taking care not to let them disintegrate. Line the bottom of a buttered heatproof dish with the bread slices, then put on a layer of sliced fruit, then another layer of bread and continue thus until the dish is full. The top layer should be bread and the pudding should be arranged to resemble a wood pile. Beat the eggs with the sugar, condensed milk and a little fresh milk, pour over the pudding, dot with butter and bake in a moderate oven for 25 minutes.

Sprinkle chopped almonds or hazelnuts over the fruit layers, to add a special touch.

Rhenish Potato Pancakes
(REIBEKUCHEN AUF RHEINISCHE ART)

Ingredients: 2–2¼ lb. (1 kg.) potatoes, 2 eggs, salt, 2–3 oz. (60–80 g.) flour, fat, cranberries.

Peel and grate the potatoes and quickly mix them with the beaten eggs, salt and sufficient flour to make a thin batter. Drain any liquid from the potatoes first. Fry pancakes in hot fat and serve with cranberry compote.

Alternatively, grate the potatoes in water, squeeze out in a cloth, add a little flour (about 8 tablespoons) and a few tablespoons of milk to give it the right consistency. Now add some finely chopped or grated onion. Serve with curd cheese flavoured with lemon juice.

Creamed Rice with Blackberries
(REISCREME MIT BROMBEEREN)

Ingredients: 5½ oz. (150 g.) rice, salt, 1¼ pt. (¾ l.) milk, 2 oz. (50–60 g.) sugar, ½ vanilla pod, 6 leaves white gelatine, ¼ pt. (⅛ l.) double cream, 1½–1¾ lb. (750 g.) blackberries, extra sugar.

Wash the rice and bring to the boil in lightly salted water. Drain, then cook the rice with the milk, sugar and vanilla until soft. Soak the gelatine briefly in cold water, remove and dissolve it in 3–4 teaspoons water in a double saucepan. Stir in the rice, after removing the vanilla pod, and continue to stir until cooled and on the point of setting. Fold in the whipped cream. Rinse a ring mould with cold water, pile in the creamed rice and place in the refrigerator. Turn out when set and fill the centre of the ring with sugared blackberries. Serve with cold vanilla custard.

Other kinds of fruit can be used similarly, or the ring can be served with a garnish of pineapple slices.

Elderberry Pudding
(HOLLERKOCH)

Ingredients: 1 lb. (500 g.) elderberries, 2 apples, 1½–3 tsp. potato flour, sugar.

Wash the elderberries and place in a saucepan with a little water. Peel, core and slice the apples, place on top of the berries and cook the fruit gently until the berries are tender. Rub the fruit through a sieve and return the pulp to the stove.

Blend the potato flour with a little cold water to a smooth paste and thicken the fruit with it. Sweeten to taste.

This sweet is highly popular in Austria with both young and old.

Fruit Dumplings
(QUARK-KNÖDEL)

Ingredients: 1½ lb. (500–750 g.) plums (switzens are best), lump sugar, salt, butter, white breadcrumbs or sugar and cinnamon.

For the pastry: 1½ lb. (750 g.) curd cheese, 3 eggs, 4½ tbsp. flour, pinch of salt, 5 tbsp. white breadcrumbs, 7 tbsp. semolina, grated lemon rind.

Put the pastry ingredients into a mixing bowl and work well together. Set aside for 1 hour. Meanwhile remove the stones from the plums and replace each with a sugar lump. Roll out the pastry on a floured board and cut into 2–2½ inch squares. Place a plum on each square, fold the pastry over and pinch the edges together carefully. Have ready a pan of boiling salted water, immerse the dumplings and allow them to simmer uncovered for 10–15 minutes. When they rise to the surface they are done. Serve hot, sprinkled with sugar and cinnamon and melted butter, or with breadcrumbs fried in butter. Serve with hot custard or fruit sauce.

Alternative fillings are blanched apricots, yellow plums or slices of pears.

Noodle Pudding with Plums
(MILCHNUDELN MIT ZWETSCHGEN)

Ingredients: ½ lb. (250 g.) noodles, 1¾ pt. (1 l.) milk, 1 oz. (30 g.) butter, 1 lb. (500 g.) plums, piece of lemon rind, sugar, cinnamon.

Bring the milk and butter to the boil in a pan. Add the noodles and simmer gently until all the milk has been absorbed and a skin has formed at the top; this should take about 40–45 minutes. In the meantime, wash and stone the plums and cook in a little water with the lemon rind and sugar to taste, taking care to keep them whole. Arrange the noodles in a serving dish, pile the fruit on top, sprinkle with sugar and cinnamon and serve.

Cheese Cream with Plums
(QUARKCREME MIT PFLAUMEN)

Ingredients: 1 lb. (500 g.) plums, sugar, ½ lb. (250 g.) curd cheese, 1½–2 tbsp. condensed milk, 1 egg yolk, 1 pkt. (1½ tbsp.) vanilla sugar.

Wash, stone and slice the plums, place them in a glass dish and sprinkle with sugar. Put aside. Cream the remaining ingredients well together until light and fluffy. Arrange the cream on top of the plums.

If tinned plums are used, these should be drained and stoned, rubbed through a sieve, and the pulp mixed with the cheese cream. The addition of 2–3 tablespoons grated hazelnuts gives more substance to this dish.

In either case, served with bread and butter this makes an enjoyable supper dish for children.

Pear Fritters
(FRUCHTKÜCHLEIN)

Ingredients: 3–4 pears, juice of 2 lemons, 9 oz. (250 g.) flour, 2 eggs, pinch of salt, scant ½ pint (¼ litre) soda water, ¾ tbsp. vegetable oil, fat, sugar, cinnamon.

Peel and core the pears and cut into round slices. Sprinkle with lemon juice. Make a batter with the flour, egg yolks, salt, soda water and oil. Beat the egg whites stiffly and fold in. Dip the pear slices into the batter and fry in deep fat until golden. Arrange the fritters on a warmed plate, sprinkle with sugar and cinnamon. Hand hot chocolate or fruit sauce round separately.

Yellow plums, grapes, sliced melons or oranges may be prepared in the same way. Instead of soda water, half milk and half water can be used.

Fruit Custard Sabine
(BREI SABINCHEN)

Ingredients per person: ⅓–½ pt. (¼ l.) milk, ¾ oz. (20 g.) potato
flour, 1¾ tbsp. sugar, 1 stewed pear,
apple or peach, a pinch of ground
cinnamon, biscuit crumbs.

Blend the potato flour with the milk, add sugar, bring to the
boil and allow to thicken, stirring all the time. Pour into a dish.
Add the fruit, ground cinnamon, and a little sugar, pour the
fruit syrup over and sprinkle with biscuit crumbs.

Jam may be used instead of stewed fruit.

Grape Soufflé Henneberg
(HENNEBERGER TRAUBENSPEISE)

Ingredients: 2–2¼ lb. (1 kg.) grapes, butter, ¾–1 pt. (½ l.) sour
cream, 4 eggs, 3½ tbsp. white breadcrumbs, grated
rind of ½ lemon, sugar, cinnamon.

Wash and dry the grapes and place in a buttered soufflé dish.
Cream the egg yolks, sugar, breadcrumbs and lemon rind.
Beat the sour cream and blend with the egg mixture. Fold in the
stiffly beaten egg whites, pile into the dish and bake in a
moderate oven for 35–45 minutes. Sprinkle with sugar and
cinnamon and serve at once.

Broken Semolina Pancakes
(GREISSCHMARREN)

Ingredients: 7 oz. (200 g.) semolina, 1¼ pt. (¾ l.) milk, 2 eggs,
pinch of salt, 3½–5 tbsp. sugar, grated rind of 1
lemon, 4½–6 oz. (125–175 g.) fat (preferably
margarine), 1 oz. (40 g.) raisins, mixed sugar and
cinnamon.

Stir the semolina into the cold milk and set aside for 45 minutes
to swell. Then add the egg yolks, salt, sugar, grated lemon rind,
raisins and finally the stiffly beaten egg whites. Heat the fat in
a frying pan and pour the mixture in. Brown on one side, turn,
brown the other side, then tear into irregularly shaped pieces.

Fry these until crisp. Arrange on a serving dish and sprinkle with sugar and cinnamon. Serve with stewed apples or other fruit.

Pancakes with Figs
(EIERKUCHEN MIT FEIGEN)

Ingredients: 9 oz. (250 g.) flour, 2–3 eggs, pinch of salt, scant ½ pt. (¼ l.) milk, 4–5 dried figs, 1 oz. (30 g.) ground almonds, fat, sugar, cinnamon.

Make a batter with the flour, egg yolks, salt and milk. Cut the figs into thin strips, add to the batter together with the almonds and finally fold in the stiffly beaten whites. Fry the pancakes in hot fat on both sides, roll up and serve sprinkled with sugar and cinnamon.

Pancake Pudding
(EIERKUCHEN-RESTESPEISE)

Ingredients: 5–6 pancakes, butter, 2 oz. (50 g.) shredded almonds, 7 oz. (200 g.) raisins or 9 oz. (250 g.) grapes, 4–8 fl. oz. (⅛–¼ l.) single cream, 2–3 eggs, grated lemon rind.

Cut the pancakes into thin strips and place them in a buttered heatproof dish. Scatter the almonds and the grapes or raisins over them. Add the beaten eggs and grated lemon rind to the cream and pour over the pancakes. Bake in a warm oven until the custard thickens. Serve with fruit compote.

Rice Pudding from Brabant
(BRABANTER REISSPEISE)

Ingredients: 7 oz. (200 g.) pudding rice, 2½ pt. (1½ l.) milk, pinch of salt, 2 egg yolks, sugar, grated lemon rind, 1½–1¾ lb. (750 g.) apples, butter, 1 stick cinnamon, mixed sugar and cinnamon.

Wash the rice and cook it in the lightly salted milk until quite soft. Leave to cool, then stir in the yolks and add sugar and grated lemon rind to taste. In the meantime, peel and core the apples, cut into pieces and cook in a little water with the cinnamon until tender. Butter a baking dish and fill it with alternate layers of rice and apples. The top layer should be rice. Dot with butter and bake in a moderate oven for 20 minutes. Serve hot with a sugar and cinnamon mixture handed separately. Fruit syrup or grated chocolate are optional accompaniments often welcomed by children.

Swabian Apple Dumplings
(SCHWÄBISCHE APFELKÜCHLE)

Ingredients: ¾ lb. (375 g.) apples, 2 oz. (60 g.) sultanas, 14–16 oz. (400–450 g.) flour, 1 tsp. baking powder, 1 egg, pinch of salt, grated rind of 1 lemon, scant ½ pt. (¼ l.) milk, 1 oz. (30 g.) butter, 3½–5 tbsp. breadcrumbs.

Peel and core the apples and cut into thin strips. Sift the flour with the baking powder, add the egg, salt, grated lemon rind and milk and beat well with a wooden spoon until the mixture begins to show bubbles. Add the apple and sultanas. Have ready a pan of salted boiling water. Dip a tablespoon into water, scoop out spoonfuls of the mixture and drop into the pan. The dumplings will rise to the surface after about 12 minutes when they are done. Lift out and arrange on a dish with breadcrumbs fried in butter.

Bread and Fruit Pudding
(OFENSCHLUPFER)

Ingredients: 6–8 stale bread rolls or an equivalent amount of white bread, 1½–1¾ lb. (750 g.) apples, grated rind of 1 lemon, sugar, 3½ oz. (100 g.) sultanas, 1¼ pt. (¾ l.) milk, 3 eggs, butter.

Slice the bread. Peel, core and slice the apples into rings, put them in a bowl and sprinkle with sugar and grated lemon rind. Wash and add the sultanas. Put alternate layers of bread and fruit into a buttered heatproof dish, with bread forming the top layer. Beat the eggs and mix with the milk and a little

175

additional sugar. Dot with butter and bake in a moderate oven for 30–40 minutes.

Fruits other than apples may be used in this dish.

Hidden Apples
(VERDECKTE ÄPFEL)

Ingredients: 2 lb. (1 kg.) apples, 1 lb. (500 g.) jam, 5 tbsp. raisins, 5 oz. (150 g.) ground almonds, 5–8 tbsp. oatmeal, 1½–2 tbsp. sugar, butter.

Peel, core and dice or slice the apples thinly. Dilute the jam with water (or wine). Place a layer of apples in a buttered heatproof dish, top with a layer of jam, sprinkled with ground almonds and some raisins. Continue in this way, finishing with a layer of jam. Sprinkle the top with a mixture of oatmeal and sugar, dot with butter and bake in a hot oven for a few minutes. Serve at once.

Apple Hedgehogs
(APFELIGEL)

Ingredients: 4 apples, juice of 1 lemon, sugar, 2 egg whites, 2–2½ oz. (50–80 g.) icing sugar, a few almonds.

Blanch the almonds and cut into spikes. Peel and core the apples and cut in half. Gently cook in a little sweetened water, taking great care not to let them get too soft. They should retain their shape. Add lemon juice, then lift the apples on to a greased baking tin. Beat the egg whites stiffly and add icing sugar. Cover each apple with some of the mixture and stick the almond spikes into the outside to give the appearance of hedgehogs. Put in a moderate oven for 5–10 minutes until the meringue is set. Arrange on a serving dish.

Alternatively, the meringue can be omitted and the hedgehogs served with chocolate sauce or whipped cream, if desired.

Apple Baskets
(APFELKÖRBCHEN)

Ingredients: 3 large juicy apples, 2 oranges, 1 oz. (30 g.) raisins, 1 oz. (30 g.) chopped almonds or hazelnuts, lemon juice, sugar.

Wash and halve the apples and scoop out the flesh, leaving a little less than $\frac{1}{2}$ inch thickness all round. Scallop the edges if desired. Peel the oranges, remove the pith and chop into small pieces. Mix with the nuts or almonds, the washed raisins and the chopped flesh of the apples. Add sugar and lemon juice and pile the mixture into the apple shells.

Top with whipped cream for festive occasions.

Little Apple Puddings
(PUDDINGKÖPFCHEN)

Ingredients: 1 lb. (500 g.) apples, 3–4 tbsp. sugar, 1 egg white, 1 pkt. (2 tbsp.) custard powder, $\frac{3}{4}$–1 pt. ($\frac{1}{2}$ l.) milk.

Slice and core the apples and cook in a little water until tender. Rub through a sieve and sweeten to taste. Make a custard with the milk and custard powder and fold in the stiffly beaten egg white. Rinse some coffee cups with cold water and fill these with alternate layers of apple pulp (which must not be too thin) and custard, beginning with a layer of custard. Leave the little puddings to set, then turn them out on to individual dishes and serve with fruit sauce or cream.

Semolina Flummery with Apples
(GRIESSFLAMMERI MIT APFELMUS)

Ingredients: $1\frac{3}{4}$ pt. (1 l.) milk, 1 oz. (30 g.) butter, $4\frac{1}{2}$ oz. (120 g.) semolina, piece of thinly pared lemon rind, 1 pkt. ($1\frac{1}{2}$ tbsp.) vanilla sugar, $1\frac{1}{2}$ oz. (40–50 g.) sugar, 2 eggs, 2–$2\frac{1}{4}$ lb. (1 kg.) apples.

Bring the milk to the boil with the butter and lemon rind, gradually add the semolina and simmer for a few minutes. Remove the lemon rind and add the sugar and vanilla sugar. When the mixture has cooled, add the beaten egg yolk and finally fold in the stiffly beaten whites. Peel and quarter the apples and stew them in a little water. Sieve and add the pulp to the flummery.

Cuckoo Apples
(KUCKUCKSÄPFEL)

Ingredients: 4 cooking apples, butter, 'boudoir' or sponge biscuits, 2½ oz. (75 g.) flour, 4 eggs, 2 oz. (60 g.) sugar, 1 pkt. (1½ tbsp.) vanilla sugar, scant ½ pt. (¼ l.) apple juice or milk.

Peel, halve and core the apples and poach them for a short time in a little apple juice. They must not become too soft. Lift them out and drain well. Butter a heatproof dish and put in a layer of biscuits. Place the apple halves on top. Mix together the flour, egg yolks, sugar and vanilla sugar and add milk or apple juice until the consistency is thick and creamy. Pour over the apples and bake in a moderate oven until set. Serve hot or cold.

Salzburg Macaroni Pudding
(SALZBURGER MACCARONISPEISE)

Ingredients: ½ lb. (250 g.) macaroni, ¾ lb. (350 g.) apples, 1½–1¾ pt. (1 l.) milk, 1 stick cinnamon, salt, sugar.

Immerse the macaroni in boiling salted water and leave to cook for a few moments. Drain. Bring the milk to the boil, add a pinch of salt, the cinnamon, then the macaroni, and simmer until done. Meanwhile peel and slice the apples thinly. Add them to the macaroni just before it is cooked. When the apples are soft, remove the cinnamon stick, mix the pudding well and serve sprinkled with sugar.

Witches' Cream
(HEXENCREME)

Ingredients: 2–2¼ lb. (1 kg.) apples, sugar, 1½ oz. (45 g.) butter, 1½–2 tbsp. white breadcrumbs, 1 oz. (30 g.) chopped almonds or hazelnuts, 2 egg whites, 1 pkt. (1½ tbsp.) vanilla sugar.

Wash and slice the apples. Bring to the boil in a little water sweetened with sugar to taste. When soft, rub them through a sieve and place the pulp, which must not be too thin, in a buttered heatproof dish. Cream 1 ounce butter, add the breadcrumbs, almonds or hazelnuts, and vanilla sugar and fold in the stiffly beaten egg whites. Spread the mixture over the apple purée and bake in a moderate oven until golden.

Shoemaker's Pudding
(SCHUSTERSPEISE)

Ingredients: 1 pkt. sponge biscuits or an equivalent amount of sponge cake, butter, apple purée, 3–4 bananas, 3 egg whites, ½ tsp. potato flour, icing sugar.

Butter a loose-bottomed cake tin (preferably of the spring type) and line the bottom with sponge biscuits or cake. Spread a 1 inch thick layer of hot apple purée on top and leave to soak in. In the case of boudoir biscuits, it should be left overnight. Now top with a layer of sliced bananas. Sweeten the stiffly beaten egg whites with icing sugar, add the potato flour and spread over the fruit. Bake in a fairly hot oven for 5 minutes until the meringue begins to brown.

Baked Apples
(BRATÄPFEL)

Ingredients: Ripe apples, sugar.

Wash and dry the apples and place them in a heatproof dish. Sprinkle generously with sugar and bake or grill.

Alternatively, the apples can be cored, filled with sugar, then baked in a dish with a little water.

Peeled baked apples served with raisin sauce (see under Fruit Sauces) make another appetizing sweet course.

Barbara's Dish
(BARBARASCHÜSSEL)

Ingredients: 4 bananas, 1–1½ lb. (450–675 g.) thick apple purée, 1 pkt. (1½ tbsp.) vanilla sugar, sugar, 2½ tsp. lemon juice, ¼ pt. (⅛ l.) double cream, 3½ tbsp. oatmeal, butter.

179

Mash the bananas with a fork and mix with the apple purée.
Flavour with lemon juice, vanilla sugar and sugar to taste
then fold in the whipped cream. Arrange on a serving dish.
Fry the oatmeal crisply in butter and use as a garnish. Serves 3.

Alternatively, arrange the bananas, apple purée and whipped
cream in separate dishes and serve with pumpernickel bread
(available in delicatessen shops) as a light and wholesome
supper dish.

Banana Fancy
(BANANEN-PHANTASIE)

Ingredients: ¾–1 pt. (½ l.) milk, 1 pkt. (2 tbsp.) custard powder,
1½–2 tbsp. sugar, 1 egg, 1 banana.

Make the custard with milk, custard powder and sugar in the
usual way. Take off the heat and stir in the egg yolk and mashed
banana. Finally, fold in the stiffly beaten egg white.

Indian Coconut Bananas
(KOKOSNUSSBANANEN AUF INDISCHE ART)

Ingredients: 4 bananas, 1 oz. (30 g.) butter, juice of 1 orange
and 1 lemon, 3½–5 tbsp. grated coconut.

Peel and halve the bananas lengthwise and place them in a
buttered heatproof dish. Sprinkle with lemon and orange
juice, then with melted butter and finally with grated coconut.
Bake in a moderate oven for 15 minutes. Serve with redcurrant,
raspberry or another fruit juice, poured over or handed round
separately.

Orange Flummery
(ORANGENFLAMMERI)

Ingredients: 1¼ pt. (¾ l.) milk, 3 oz. (90 g.) semolina, 5 tbsp.
sugar, 1 egg, pinch of salt, grated rind of 1 orange,
juice of 2 oranges, 3½ tbsp. grated chocolate, 2–3
tbsp. orange marmalade.

Bring the milk to the boil, stir in the semolina, sugar and salt,
reduce the heat and simmer for a few moments. Remove from

180

the stove, add the egg yolk, the orange juice and rind and lastly fold in stiffly beaten egg white. Arrange the flummery in a serving dish, leave to cool, then sprinkle with the grated chocolate and decorate with dots of marmalade.

Baked Orange Slices
(GEBACKENE ORANGENSCHEIBEN)

Ingredients: 5–6 eggs, ½ lb. (250 g.) flour, pinch of salt, milk, 4 oranges, fat, sugar.

Prepare a pancake batter from the eggs, flour and salt, adding a little milk if necessary. Peel and slice the oranges, dip in the batter and fry in deep fat. Sprinkle with sugar and serve at once.

Children's Dream
(KINDERTRAUM)

Ingredients: 4 oz. (125 g.) pudding rice, piece of butter, juice of 4 oranges and 1 lemon, 2½ oz. (80 g.) sugar, ¼ pt. (⅛ l.) double cream, 1 banana, 1 orange.

Boil the rice in plenty of water with a piece of butter added, until tender. Drain off any water not absorbed. Add the fruit juices and sugar, then fold in the whipped cream. Decorate with banana and orange slices.

Quince Croquettes
(QUITTENKROKETTEN)

Ingredients: 3¼–3½ lb. (1½ kg.) ripe quinces, sugar, grated rind of 1 lemon, 2 egg yolks, soft white bread-crumbs, fat, cinnamon.

Brush and chop the quinces, cook in a little water, then rub through a sieve. Sweeten the fruit pulp with sugar to taste, flavour with grated lemon rind and add sufficient breadcrumbs to form croquettes. Dip these in beaten yolk, then in bread-crumbs and fry crisply in plenty of fat. Sprinkle with sugar and cinnamon and serve hot with vanilla custard.

Rice Pudding with Mixed Fruit
(BUNTER MILCHREIS)

Ingredients: 4 oz. (125 g.) pudding rice, 1¼ pt. (¾ l.) milk, grated rind of ½ lemon, 1¾ oz. (50 g.) sugar, pinch of salt, 3 leaves white gelatine, 1 lb. (500 g.) mixed fresh fruit or tinned fruit salad, mixed sugar and cinnamon.

Wash the rice, put it in a pan with plenty of water and bring to the boil. Drain. Put the rice back into the pan with the milk, sugar, grated lemon rind and salt and simmer until the rice is quite soft. Dissolve the gelatine in a double saucepan, stir into the rice and leave to cool. Chop the fresh fruit or drain the tinned. Arrange the rice and fruit in layers in a serving dish and serve sprinkled with sugar and cinnamon.

Potato Crumble
(KARTOFFELSTERZ)

Ingredients: 2–2¼ lb. (1 kg.) boiled potatoes, 7 oz. (200 g.) flour, salt, fat.

Grate the potatoes, add the flour and a little salt and work well together. Crumble the mixture on to a greased baking tin with both hands and bake in a hot oven for a few minutes. Tear apart with two forks and pile on a serving dish. Serve with fruit sauce or compote.

Stuttgart Curd Cheese Pudding
(STUTTGARTER QUARKAUFLAUF)

Ingredients: 1½ oz. (45 g.) butter, 8 tbsp. sugar, 2–3 eggs, 1 lb. (500 g.) curd cheese, grated rind and juice of ½ lemon, 1¾ oz. (50 g.) potato flour, ½ tsp. baking powder, 1 lb. (500 g.) stewed pears or stewed or puréed apples.

Cream 1 ounce (30 grammes) butter, the sugar, and egg yolks together until quite smooth. Add the curd cheese, lemon rind and juice, potato flour and baking powder, and fold in the stiffly beaten egg whites. Pile alternate layers of the cheese mixture and fruit into a buttered soufflé dish and bake in a moderate oven for 30 minutes.

Summer Refreshments

FRUIT JUICES

All types of fruit juice can be made into refreshing drinks which
are especially welcome during the hot season of the year. Have
the juice ready in suitable glasses and top up with iced water or,
better still, well-chilled soda water, just before serving. Icing
sugar is preferable to ordinary sugar as a sweetener because it
dissolves more quickly.

Mixed Fruit Drink
(FRUCHTSAFT-MISCHGETRÄNK)
Ingredients: Apple juice, lemon juice, sugar, soda water.
Fill the glasses three-quarters full of apple juice. Add lemon
juice, sweeten with sugar and top up with soda water.

Summer Fruit Drink
(SOMMERDRINK)
Ingredients: $\frac{1}{2}$ lb. (250 g.) mixed fruit (strawberries, raspberries, mandarin oranges, pineapple), 3 tbsp.
sugar, $\frac{1}{2}$ pt. ($\frac{1}{4}$–$\frac{3}{8}$ l.) any fruit juice or syrup, soda
water, vanilla ice cream.

Clean and prepare the fruit, chopping it up if necessary, sprinkle with sugar and set aside until the sugar is absorbed. Divide the fruit between 3 tall glasses, add fruit juice or syrup and top up with soda water. Add a portion of ice cream, if desired. Hand round cocktail sticks or small spoons for picking out the fruit. Serves 3.

Fizzy Drink
(PERLDRINK)

Ingredients: 2–2¼ lb. (1 kg.) redcurrants, sugar, soda water, ice cubes.

Wash the berries and rub them through a sieve. Sweeten the resulting juice to taste. Pour into a bottle, seal and leave for a day. Serve in wide glasses topped with soda water and add an ice cube to each glass.

Strawberries, raspberries and gooseberries may be used in a similar way.

Gooseberry Fruit Drink
(STACHELBEER-DRINK)

Ingredients: 1–1¼ lb. (500 g.) gooseberries, 7 oz. (200 g.) sugar, rind of ½ lemon, soda water, condensed milk.

Prepare and wash the gooseberries and put them in a pan with the sugar, lemon rind and a scant ½ pint (¼ litre) water. Cook, then strain through a sieve. Put 2–3 tablespoons fruit pulp into each glass, add a little condensed milk and top up with soda water.

Alternatively, omit the milk and top each glass with whipped cream.

Peach Aperitif
(PFIRSICH APERITIF)

Ingredients: 4 ripe peaches, gin, soda water.

Wash, peel and stone the peaches, rub through a sieve or put in the electric blender. Pour the juice into 4 cocktail glasses, add gin and top up with iced soda water.

Orange or lemon juice may be used in the same way.

Fruit Champagne
(FRUCHTSEKT)

Ingredients: 1 banana, 1 orange, 3–4 pineapple rings, a few cherries, 2–3 tbsp. sugar, 1–2 bottles white wine, 1–1½ bottles soda water.

Peel the banana and oranges, chop all the fruit, place in a deep bowl and sprinkle with sugar. When some juice has formed pour over the wine and leave to stand in a cool place for several hours. Add the soda water at the last moment and serve in champagne glasses. Serve ice cubes separately.

Children's Joy
(FRUCHTSAFT KINDERGLÜCK)

Ingredients: Juice of 1 lemon per glass, raspberry syrup, soda water.

Fill each glass to one third with syrup, add the lemon juice and top up with soda water.

In summer, add an ice cube and serve with drinking straws.

Apple Sherbet
(APFELSAFT SORBET)

Ingredients: ¾–1 pt. (½ l.) apple juice, ½–1 pt. (⅜–⅝ l.) fruit syrup (strawberry, raspberry or pear), soda water, 3 tbsp. fresh berries.

Half fill each glass with apple juice. Add fruit syrup and stir well. Top with soda water and a few berries.

Orange Tea
(ORANGENTEE)

Stir ¾ teaspoon fresh orange juice into ½ pint (¼ litre) strong, sweet tea.

This makes an aromatic and refreshing pick-me-up in hot weather.

Lemon Syrup
(ZITRONENSIRUP)

Ingredients: 6 lemons, 1 lb. (500 g.) sugar, 1¼ oz. (38 g.) citric
acid crystals (obtainable from chemists), soda
water.

Wash and dry the lemons and grate the rind. Put the grated
rind into a bowl with the sugar and citric acid. Add 2 pints
(1⅛ litres) water, stir well, cover and leave to stand for 3 days,
stirring occasionally. Then decant the syrup into bottles. Keep
firmly stoppered. When a refreshing and thirst-quenching
drink is required for children and guests, pour a small quantity into a glass and top up with soda water.

Orange syrup may be produced in the same way.

**Cold and Hot Lemonade and Orangeade from Grandmother's
Cookbook**

Take 2 lemons and 2 ounces (50 grammes) lump sugar. Grate
the lemon rind over the sugar, squeeze the juice and pour over
the sugar also. When the sugar has dissolved pour on 1 pint
(⅝ litre) cold or boiling water and strain the liquid through a
piece of muslin. Do not use the grated rind if the lemonade is
being made for an invalid. Use oranges in a similar way to
prepare a well-flavoured drink called orangeade.

Elderberry Lemonade
(HOLUNDERLIMONADE)

Ingredients: 1¾ lb. (750 g.) sugar, 9 lemons, 2 wine glasses
vinegar, 3–4 elderflowers, 10 grains rice.

Place the sugar in a deep bowl and pour 17½ pints (10 litres)
water over. Wash the elderflowers and add, together with the
sliced lemons and vinegar. Cover with a cloth and leave to
stand in a warm room for 4–5 days, stirring the mixture occasionally. Have ready some well washed bottles (soda water
bottles with spring tops are best). Strain the liquid through a
fine sieve or muslin and decant into the bottles. Distribute the
grains of rice between the bottles. Keep them standing up in a
cool place for 2 weeks when the lemonade will be ready.

The following drinks will all be great favourites with children. When served to adults each can be improved by a dash of brandy. Milk drinks should be served in tall glasses and drinking straws handed round with them. A few berries or pieces of fruit floating on top give a gay appearance to the drinks. Biscuits, waffles or plain cake may be served as an accompaniment.

Swedish Milk
(SCHWEDENMILCH)

Ingredients: ½ pt. (¼ l.) fresh berry juice (strawberries, raspberries, currants), sugar, ¼ pt. (⅛ l.) sweetened cream, fresh berries.

Mix the ingredients and pour into tall glasses. Top with a few fresh berries.

Add a tablespoon vermouth, if desired. Serves two.

Strawberry Milk
(ERDBEERMILCH)

Ingredients: 1 lb. (500 g.) strawberries, 1¼ pt. (¾ l.) milk, ½ pt. (¼–⅛ l.) sweetened condensed milk, 1–2 pkt. (1½–3 tbsp.) vanilla sugar, grated rind of 1 lemon.

Hull and wash the strawberries, then rub through a sieve or put in the blender. Flavour the chilled milk with vanilla sugar. Mix with the fruit purée, pour into glasses, top with condensed milk and sprinkle with grated lemon rind.

Strawberry Ice Cubes
(ERDBEER-EISWÜRFEL)

Ingredients: 3–7 oz. (100–200 g.) strawberries, milk, vanilla sugar.

Wash and hull the strawberries. Place one strawberry in each compartment of the freezing tray of the refrigerator, sweeten milk with vanilla sugar and pour on top of the strawberries. Leave to freeze.

Add one or two strawberry ice cubes to glasses of milk, vermouth or cocktails.

Fruit Milk
(FRUCHTMILCH)

Ingredients per person: 2–3 tbsp. strawberries or raspberries, 1 apricot or peach, 1½–2 tsp. sugar, milk.

Clean the berries, mash with a fork and place in glasses. Blanch, stone and mash the other fruit and put on top. Sweeten. Fill the glasses with chilled milk and serve. Hand each person a spoon to stir the drink, if desired.

Raspberry Milk
(HIMBEERMILCH)

Ingredients per person: 4 oz. (125 g.) raspberries, 2½ tsp. condensed milk or cream, milk.

Set aside 5–6 raspberries and make a purée from the rest. Mix the pulp with cream or condensed milk, put in a glass, then fill it with milk. Garnish with the whole fruit.

The pure fruit pulp mixed with soda water makes an equally refreshing, simple drink.

Peach Milk Elizabeth
(PFIRSICH-MILCH ELISABETH)

Ingredients: 3 ripe peaches, ½ pt. (¼ l.) raspberry juice, 1 pt. (½ l.) milk, 2 pkt. (3 tbsp.) vanilla sugar.

Blanch, stone and chop the peaches. Pour the raspberry juice over and leave to stand for a while. Finally add the vanilla-flavoured milk.

Quick Milk Shake
(OBSTSAFT-BLITZGETRÄNK)

Ingredients: Fruit juice, ½ pkt. (¾ tbsp.) vanilla sugar, ¼–½ pt. (⅛–¼ l.) milk, 1 tsp. grated nuts.

Fill one-third of a glass with fruit juice, add vanilla sugar, chilled milk and nuts and stir well.

In hot weather add an ice cube.

Vitamin Shake
(VITAMIN–SHAKE)

Ingredients: ½ pt. (¼ l.) milk, 2 tbsp. grapefruit juice, 1–2 tbsp. sea buckthorn syrup.

Add the grapefruit juice slowly, drop by drop, to the milk, stirring vigorously. Add the buckthorn syrup, stir or shake and serve. Serves two.

Orange Milk
(ORANGENMILCH)

Ingredients per person: Juice of 1 orange, ¼ pt. (⅛ l.) milk, 1½ tsp. sugar, 1 portion vanilla ice cream, grated orange rind.

Add the orange juice to the milk very slowly. Mash the ice cream with a fork and add it to the milk together with the sugar. Sprinkle grated orange rind on top and serve.

Omit the ice cream and add a dash of vermouth to make a delicious cocktail.

Hawaii-Drink

Ingredients: 10–11 oz. (300 g.) strawberries, ¼ pt. (⅛ l.) tinned pineapple juice, 1¼ pt. (⅔ l.) milk, 1 pkt. (1½ tbsp.) vanilla sugar, sugar, pineapple pieces.

Mash two-thirds of the strawberries and thin the pulp with the pineapple juice. Add the milk and vanilla sugar and sweeten to taste. Chill. Serve with a garnish of whole strawberries and pineapple pieces.

Yogurt Shake
(JOGHURT-SHAKE)

Ingredients: ½ pt. (¼ l.) fruit juice, ¼ pt. (⅛ l.) yogurt, ½ pt. (¼ l.) milk, 1 tsp. lemon juice, sugar.

Mix the ingredients well together and sweeten to taste. Serves two.

Blackcurrant Shake
(SCHWARZER JOHANNISBEERTRUNK)

Ingredients: 4 oz. (125 g.) blackcurrants, $\frac{1}{4}$–$\frac{1}{2}$ pt. ($\frac{1}{4}$ l.) buttermilk or yogurt, sugar, $2\frac{1}{2}$ tsp. brandy.

Sieve the blackcurrants and mix the juice with the buttermilk
or yogurt. Add the brandy and sugar to taste. Serves two.

FRUIT CUPS

Presentation and decoration are particularly important when
it comes to fruit cups. The aim is to attract the eye by the
judicious use of tasteful garnishes such as whole fruit, pralines,
flaked chocolate, truffles, etc. Candied fruit can look attractive,
too.

Where a recipe for home-made ice cream contains fruit,
the fruit should be soaked in brandy for a short time first
wherever possible. This process preserves softness and prevents
freezing. Frozen fruits tend to lose some of their flavour. On
the other hand, a dash of alcohol enhances the flavour of the
finished dish.

Strawberry Request Cup
(ERDBEERWUNSCH-BECHER)

Ingredients: 1 lb. (500 g.) strawberries, 3 tbsp. brandy, 8 fl.
oz. ($\frac{1}{4}$ l.) double cream, 1 pkt. ($1\frac{1}{2}$ tbsp.) vanilla
sugar, 7 tbsp. sugar, grated chocolate, mandarin
or pineapple pieces.

Clean, hull and rub half the strawberries through a sieve.
Mix the fruit pulp with the whipped cream, half the sugar and
the vanilla sugar. Pile the cream mixture into ice trays, switch
the refrigerator to its lowest temperature and leave to freeze.
Meanwhile, hull the remaining strawberries, put them in a
dish, sprinkle with sugar and pour the brandy over. Cover and
set aside. When the cream has set, place it in champagne
glasses, arrange the strawberries on top, garnish with mandarin or pineapple pieces and sprinkle with grated chocolate.

Strawberry Ice Cream
(ERDBEER-ICE-CREAM)

Ingredients: 1 lb. (500 g.) strawberries, 1½ oz. (50 g.) grated
hazelnuts, 1½ oz. (50 g.) grated chocolate, 8 fl. oz.
(¼ l.) double cream, 5 tsp. sugar.

Wash, hull and chop the strawberries. Add the chocolate and
hazelnuts and fold in the whipped cream. Put the mixture
into ice trays, set the refrigerator at the lowest temperature
and freeze for 2 hours.

Sprinkle with 2½ teaspoons brandy for extra flavour.

Ice Cream Slices with Strawberries
(EISSCHNITTEN MIT ERDBEEREN)

Ingredients per person: 1 slice vanilla or chocolate ice cream,
strawberries, sugar, double cream.

Wash, hull and chop the strawberries. Sprinkle with sugar and
mix with the whipped cream. Place an ice cream slice on each
dish, top with the fruit mixture and garnish with whole
strawberries. Serve at once.

Bavarian Raspberry Cup
(HIMBEER-BECHER TITISEE)

Ingredients per person: 2–3 tbsp. ice cream (hazelnut, fruit or
vanilla), 4 oz. (125 g.) sugared rasp-
berries, double cream, cocoa or grated
chocolate.

Place the ice cream in champagne glasses or glass dishes, top
with fruit and garnish with whipped cream. Sprinkle with
cocoa or chocolate.

Redcurrant Cup
(JOHANNISBEER-COUPÉ)

Ingredients: 7 oz. (200 g.) redcurrants, 2 egg yolks, 1 egg white,
5–7 tbsp. icing sugar, 1¼ pt. (¾ l.) milk.

Wash the fruit and put in the electric blender or rub through a
fine sieve. Mix with the egg yolks and icing sugar. Put the

fruit mixture into glasses, add the milk and stir well. Crown
each portion with a spoonful of stiffly beaten egg white and
decorate with a cluster of redcurrants.

Mixed Fruit Cup
(FRÜCHTEBECHER)

Ingredients: ¾ lb. (375 g.) mixed fruit, sugar, 2–3 tbsp. brandy,
4 portions vanilla ice cream, double cream.

Wash the fruit, chop if necessary, mix with sugar and pour
over the brandy. Cover and set aside. Just before serving
place the fruit in glasses, add a layer of ice cream, repeat the
two layers and top with whipped cream.

Iceberg
(EISBERG)

Ingredients: 3–4 peaches, 3½ tbsp. condensed milk, ½ pt. (¼–⅜ l.)
raspberry juice, milk, soda water, ice cubes or
vanilla ice cream.

Blanch and stone the peaches, purée in an electric blender or
with a fork and place the fruit in glasses. Add the condensed
milk and raspberry juice and stir well. Fill the glasses with
well chilled milk and top with soda water. Add ice cream or
just an ice cube.

A dash of brandy in each glass makes the drink something
special.

Pineapple on Ice
(ANANAS AUF EIS)

Ingredients: 4 portions vanilla ice cream, 4 pineapple rings,
3½ oz. (100 g.) grated chocolate, 3 tbsp. milk,
5 tsp. sugar, 4 blanched almonds.

Place a portion of ice cream in each dish or glass and top
with a chilled pineapple ring. Put the dishes in the refrigerator
and prepare the chocolate sauce in the following way: bring
the milk to the boil with the chocolate and sugar and cook for
a few moments. Pour the hot sauce over the pineapple and
serve decorated with an almond.

Banana Ice
(BANANENEIS)

Ingredients: 1–2 egg yolks, 2 oz. (60 g.) sugar, 1 banana, $\frac{3}{4}$ tsp. lemon juice, 8 fl. oz. ($\frac{1}{4}$ l.) double cream.

Beat the yolks with the sugar and lemon juice and add the mashed banana. Fold in the whipped cream and pile the mixture in the freezing tray of the refrigerator. Freeze for 3 hours at lowest temperature.

Other kinds of fruit purée can be used in the same way.

Fruit Sauces

Rhubarb Sauce
(RHABARBERSAUCE ZU RINDFLEISCH)

Ingredients: 2 oz. (60 g.) butter, 8–10 tbsp. flour, 1–1½ pt. ($\frac{5}{8}$–$\frac{7}{8}$ l.) water or unsalted stock, lemon juice, sugar, thick rhubarb compote.

Make a light roux with the butter and flour. Slowly, and stirring constantly, add the water or stock, flavour to taste with lemon juice and a little sugar, then add the rhubarb.

This sauce makes an excellent accompaniment to boiled beef or other meat.

Strawberry Sauce
(ERDBEERSAUCE)

Ingredients: ½–1 lb. (250–500 g.) strawberries, sugar, ½ stick cinnamon, 1–2 sponge biscuits.

Wash and hull the strawberries, place in a pan with sugar, the cinnamon and a little water added. Bring to the boil and cook until the strawberries are quite soft. Remove the cinnamon, strain the fruit through a sieve and add grated biscuit, the amount depending on the consistency required.

A little cream or white wine may be added to improve the sauce.

Cherry Sauce
(STETTENER KIRSCHENSAUCE)

Ingredients: 4½ oz. (125 g.) morello cherries, 7 oz. (200 g.)
sweet cherries, grated rind of ½ lemon, ½ stick
cinnamon, 1 clove, ¼ pt. (⅛ l.) red wine, ¾ tsp.
potato flour.

Stone the cherries and put through the mincer or pound in a
mortar. Bring the pulp to the boil with lemon rind, cinnamon,
clove, wine and about ¼ pint (⅛ litre) water. Simmer for half
an hour, then strain through a sieve. Make a paste with the
potato flour and a little water, stir into the sauce, return it to
the stove and let thicken. Dilute with more wine as required
or with the juices from the roasting tin.

This sauce makes a particularly delicious accompaniment
with roast duck, turkey or game. Alternatively, omit the
gravy, add sugar and serve with puddings.

Redcurrant Sauce
(JOHANNISBEERSAUCE)

Ingredients: 1 lb. (500 g.) redcurrants, 3–5 oz. (100–150 g.)
sugar, grated lemon rind, ½ stick cinnamon,
1 tbsp. potato flour.

Wash and prepare the redcurrants and cook with the sugar,
lemon rind and cinnamon in a scant ½ pint (¼ litre) water.
Strain. Thicken the juice with the potato flour.

Alternatively, sieve the fruit raw, dilute the pulp with a
scant ½ pint (¼ litre) water, bring to the boil with the sugar,
lemon rind and cinnamon, then thicken with the potato flour.

Fruit Sauce Duet
(FRUCHTSAUCE DUETT)

Ingredients: ½–¾ pt. (¼–½ l.) redcurrant juice, ½ pt. (¼–⅜ l.)
tinned pineapple juice, ¾ tsp. potato flour, brandy
or white wine.

Mix the juices, bring to the boil and thicken with potato
flour. Dilute with brandy or white wine, if desired.

Three-Fruits Sauce
(DREIFRUCHTE-SAUCE)

Ingredients: 5 oz. (150 g.) each of gooseberries, redcurrants and raspberries, sugar, lemon rind, 1 stick cinnamon, 2 cloves, 1½–2 tsp. potato flour.

Prepare the fruit and cook with sugar, lemon rind, cinnamon and cloves in ¾–1 pint (½ litre) water. Strain and thicken the juice with potato flour.

Gooseberry Wine Sauce
(STACHELBEERSCHAUMSAUCE)

Ingredients: ¾–1 pt. (½ l.) gooseberry juice, 2 eggs, 1½–2 tsp. potato flour, sugar, 1 glass white wine.

To prepare gooseberry juice, poach gooseberries in sweetened water, then sieve. Thicken the juice with potato flour in the usual way, stir in the beaten eggs and sugar, then whisk over a low heat until the mixture foams. Add the wine.

This delicious sauce combines well with puddings and flummeries. Other juices, such as redcurrant, can be used similarly.

Sauce Ostende
(OSTENDER SAUCE)

Ingredients: 1 lb. (500 g.) green gooseberries, ½ pt. (¼–⅜ l.) apple purée, lemon juice, sugar.

Prepare and wash the gooseberries, cook in water, then strain. Mix with the apples, and flavour with lemon juice and sugar. Beat well with a wire whisk.

Serve this sweet-and-sour sauce with boiled beef or pasta dishes.

Raspberry Sauce
(HIMBEER-SAUCE)

Ingredients: 1–1½ lb. (500–700 g.) raspberries (wild ones are best), thinly pared rind of ½ lemon, sugar, 1½–3 tsp. potato flour.

Clean the raspberries, then rub through a fine sieve. Sweeten the juice, add the lemon rind, bring to the boil and thicken with the potato flour. Remove the rind and leave to cool.

Serve with puddings, soufflés or creams.

Apricot Sauce
(APRIKOSEN-SAUCE)

Ingredients: 1 lb. (500 g.) apricots, ¾–1 pt. (½ l.) milk, 1 pkt. (2 tbsp.) custard powder, 3½ tbsp. sugar, ½ vanilla pod.

Stone and chop the apricots, bring to the boil in ¾–1 pint (½ litre) water. Cook until soft then rub through a sieve. Make the custard, adding sugar and the vanilla pod. Then add the apricot juice. Dilute as required.

South Tyrolean Grape Sauce
(TRAUBENSAUCE AUS SÜDTIROL)

Ingredients: 2 oz. (60 g.) butter, 1½–2 tbsp. flour, ¾–1 pt. (½ l.) white wine, 3 tbsp. cream or top of the milk, juice of 1 orange or 1 lemon, pinch of salt, pepper, 10–15 white grapes.

Make a roux with the butter and flour. When it begins to colour add the wine, then the cream or top of the milk, and season. Add the halved, peeled and seeded grapes and leave to simmer in the sauce for a short time.

This sauce tastes delicious served with sweet rice dishes and puddings. It can be used with equal success as an accompaniment to fish dishes, e.g. fried or poached fillets of sole.

Sweet Raisin Sauce
(ROSINEN-SAUCE, SÜSS)

Ingredients: ¾–1 pt. (½ l.) milk, 1 pkt. (2 tbsp.) custard powder, 2–3 tbsp. sugar, 2 oz. (50 g.) raisins, ½ tsp. rum essence, 8 blanched and shredded almonds.

Make the custard with the milk and custard powder, add the sugar and raisins and cook for a short time. Take off the stove and stir in the rum essence and almonds.

Savoury Raisin Sauce
(ROSINEN-SAUCE ZU RINDFLEISCH)

Ingredients: 2 oz. (60 g.) fat, 7 tbsp. flour, $\frac{3}{4}$–1 pt. ($\frac{1}{2}$ l.) stock or water, $2\frac{1}{2}$ oz. (50–75 g.) raisins, salt, sugar, lemon juice, red wine, 4–6 blanched and shredded almonds.

Wash the raisins, soak in water for a short time, then drain. Melt the fat in a pan, add the flour and make a fairly dark roux. Add the stock or water and raisins and simmer. Season just before serving, adding a dash of red wine if desired, and sprinkle with the almonds.

This is a popular sauce in Northern Germany where it is served with boiled beef, pork, tongue, etc. Slices of the cooked meat are put in the sauce and simmered for 10 minutes before seasoning. When water is used as the liquid, the sauce can be served with puddings also.

Fruit Foam Sauce
(FRUCHTSCHAUM-SAUCE)

Ingredients: $\frac{1}{2}$ pt. ($\frac{1}{4}$ l.) fruit juice, 6 oz. (170 g.) sugar, 1 egg white.

Put all the ingredients into a bowl and whisk until stiff.

This is a particularly versatile sauce which can be served equally successfully with fresh or stewed fruit salads or compotes or fruit which has been marinated in brandy first.

Banana Sauce
(BANANENSAUCE)

Ingredients: 2 oz. (60 g.) butter or margarine, 5 tsp. flour, scant $\frac{1}{2}$ pt. ($\frac{1}{4}$ l.) milk, juice of 1 lemon or $1\frac{3}{4}$ tsp. French mustard, pinch of sugar, $\frac{3}{4}$ tsp. tomato ketchup, $1\frac{1}{2}$ bananas, Madeira.

Make a roux of the flour and melted butter or margarine. Add milk and ketchup and cook. Flavour with sugar and lemon juice or mustard and add the mashed banana. Add a dash of Madeira wine, if desired.

Serve with slices of hard-boiled eggs or cold meat.

199

Banana Cheese Sauce
(BANANEN-QUARK-SAUCE)

Ingredients: 4 oz. (100 g.) curd cheese, 5 tbsp. condensed milk
or cream, $3\frac{1}{2}$–5 tsp. sugar, $\frac{1}{2}$ banana.

Add the milk or cream and sugar to the cheese and stir until
smooth. Mash the banana with a fork and add the purée to
the cheese mixture.

Serve with halved peaches or pears, sliced pineapple or soft
fruit. For a more delicate flavour, substitute Gervais or cream
cheese for the curd cheese.

Pineapple Sauce
(ANANASSAUCE)

Ingredients: $\frac{1}{2}$ pt. ($\frac{1}{4}$ l.) pineapple juice, $\frac{1}{2}$ oz. (15 g.) potato
flour, $\frac{1}{2}$ pt. ($\frac{1}{4}$ l.) white wine, $3\frac{1}{2}$ tsp. sugar.

Add a little juice to the potato flour, mix smoothly and thicken
the remaining juice with it. Take off the heat, add the wine and
sweeten to taste.

Florida Sauce

Ingredients: $1\frac{1}{2}$ oz. (40 g.) butter, $1\frac{1}{2}$ oz. (40 g.) flour, $\frac{1}{2}$ pt. ($\frac{1}{4}$ l.)
milk, $\frac{1}{2}$ pt. ($\frac{1}{4}$ l.) water or stock, 1 cooking apple,
2–3 tsp. curry powder, pineapple pieces or 2–3
rings, pineapple syrup.

Make a light roux with the flour and fat and blend in the milk
and stock or water. Cook for a few moments, then add the
curry powder, grated apple and pineapple pieces. Flavour with
the pineapple syrup.

Sweet Orange Sauce
(ORANGENSAUCE ZU PUDDINGS, AUFLÄUFEN UND REISSPEISEN)

Ingredients: Scant $\frac{1}{2}$ pt. ($\frac{1}{4}$ l.) milk, $1\frac{3}{4}$ tsp. potato flour, $1\frac{1}{2}$–2
tsp. sugar, juice of 4 oranges, grated rind of
1 orange.

Make a paste from the potato flour and a little milk, add the
paste to the remaining milk, bring it to the boil and let thicken.

Add the sugar, remove from the heat and stir in the orange juice and grated rind.

Serve hot or cold with puddings, soufflés and sweet rice dishes.

Savoury Orange Sauce
(ORANGENSAUCE ZU WILD, GEFLÜGEL UND KALBFLEISCH)

Ingredients: Juice of 4 oranges, 1½–2 tsp. potato flour, ¾–1 pt. (½ l.) white wine, pinch of sugar, 3 blanched and shredded almonds.

Mix the potato flour with a little orange juice to a smooth paste. Add the paste to the remaining orange juice, bring to the boil and allow to thicken. Remove from the heat and add the wine, sugar and almonds.

Serve with game, poultry and white meats.

Spanish Egg Sauce
(SPANISCHE EIERSAUCE)

Ingredients: 4 egg yolks, salt, 1 oz. (30 g.) butter, juice of 1 orange, grated rind of ½ orange, vinegar.

Whisk the yolks, with a pinch of salt added, over hot water in a double saucepan. Gradually add the butter, the orange juice and grated rind. Season with vinegar to taste.

Serve with asparagus or roast poultry.

Petersburg Fruit Sauce
(PETERSBURGER OBSTSAUCE ZU GEFLÜGEL)

Ingredients: ½ pt. (¼–⅜ l.) white wine, juice of 2 lemons or oranges, stock, 1 apple, 6 slices orange.

Heat the wine and add the juice, stock, grated apple and finely chopped orange. Keep hot.

Serve separately with roast poultry dishes.

Sweet-and-Sour Wine Sauce
(PIKANTE BRATENSAUCE MIT WEIN UND OBSTSÄFTEN)

Ingredients: Juice and grated rind of ½ orange, grated rind of ½ lemon, ¼ pt. (⅛ l.) red wine, scant ¼ pt. (⅛ l.) meat juices from the roasting tin, 1¾ tsp. French mustard, 1½–2 tbsp. redcurrant jelly, 5 grapes.

Bring the wine to the boil with the grated rinds and halved grapes and simmer for 5 minutes. Strain. Reheat the meat juices, add the wine, orange juice, mustard and jelly.

Serve this piquant sauce hot with meat dishes.

Cumberland Sauce

Ingredients: 1¾ tbsp. dry mustard, 1 glass red wine, grated rind of ½ orange, juice of 1 orange, ½ lb. (230 g.) redcurrant jelly.

Stir a little wine into the mustard, make a smooth paste, then add the remaining wine and the other ingredients. Rub through a sieve.

Serve with game, roast poultry, cold meats or grills.

Sauce Valentin

Ingredients: 1 pt. (⅝ l.) milk, 3½ tsp. potato flour, sugar, 1 pkt. (1½ tbsp.) vanilla sugar, 1 egg yolk, juice of 2 lemons.

Place the potato flour, egg yolk, sugar and vanilla sugar in a bowl and make a smooth paste with a little of the milk. Bring the remainder of the milk to the boil, pour over the mixture and stir. Flavour with lemon juice.

Serve with fresh fruit, puddings, flummeries, jellies or cream.

Substitute a pinch of salt for the sugar and season with ½ teaspoon paprika to make a sauce that will accompany chicken, fish and veal dishes.

Nutmeg Sauce
(INGWERSAUCE)

Ingredients: 2½–3 oz. (80 g.) sugar, ¼ oz. (10 g.) ground nutmeg, juice and grated rind of ½ lemon, juice of ½ orange, ¼ pt. (⅛ l.) cider.

Mix the sugar with the nutmeg, pour on a scant ½ pint (¼ litre) water and add the grated rind. Heat and simmer for 20 minutes. Strain through a fine sieve and flavour with the fruit juices and cider.

Serve with rice puddings or soufflés.

Rosehip Sauce
(HAGEBUTTENSAUCE)

Ingredients: 4 oz. (125 g.) rosehips, ¾–1 pt. (½ l.) white wine,
2–3 tbsp. sugar, pinch of ground cinnamon,
potato flour, brandy.

Top and tail the rosehips, wash and chop, then cook until
tender in a good ¾ pint (½ litre) water (about 20 minutes).
Rub through a sieve and add the wine to the pulp. Flavour
with the sugar and cinnamon, reheat and simmer for another
15 minutes. Thicken with a little potato flour if the sauce is too
thin. Finally, add brandy.

A similar sauce can be made quickly from rosehip jam.
Dilute the jam with wine, bring to the boil and thicken with
potato flour as required. Sweeten to taste and flavour with a
pinch of cinnamon and ground cloves.

Cooking for Invalids

The low calorie content of many kinds of fruit is important when considering special diets for certain ailments. In the case of obesity, good results are often achieved with a diet in which fruit only is taken by the patient on certain days, although such a diet should only be undertaken under medical supervision. A régime of fruit only is often prescribed for ailments of the heart, liver and gall bladder. Upsets of the alimentary tract and even diabetes can be alleviated with fruit diets. Light fruit dishes will often be acceptable in sickrooms from which more substantial fare is automatically excluded.

Diarrhoea in children often responds to a diet of grated raw apples, which must, however, be given for several days; dried cranberries are useful for the same purpose for both children and adults. The laxative effect of prunes is well known and 5–10 prunes, eaten first thing each morning, will ensure regular bowel movements; if preferred, the fruit can be soaked in water overnight. Gooseberries also stimulate the bowels.

Fruit is also recommended in cases of gout and rheumatism (cranberries should be excluded from the list as they stimulate the production of uric acid). Grapes, on the other hand, are beneficial to rheumatic patients as well as to sufferers from kidney and bladder diseases. When catering for a patient with a delicate stomach, it is often wise to peel and seed grapes to make them more digestible.

Coughs and catarrhal colds in children – and adults – can be alleviated with such well tried remedies as raspberry juice sweetened with honey, hot milk with honey, honey with onion juice or hot lemon juice.

Pear juice has a stimulating effect on the kidneys and can be given neat or used as a sweetener with other fruit juices. Pineapple juice will often be found to be tolerated by patients who react to other kinds of fruit with skin rashes. Pure grape juice can be included in any diet; it even has a calming effect on the nervous system. Home-made fruit juices, especially raspberry and redcurrant, have a refreshing effect on feverish patients.

FRUIT IN THE SICKROOM

Patients confined to bed often suffer from a diminished appetite and special care should be taken over the preparation and presentation of food. Vegetarian dishes and fruit soufflés should be included in such a diet, unless forbidden by the doctor, as they are easily digested. Dishes should be decorated with slices of fruit, as the colour factor plays a part in stimulating the appetite. Where the ingredients in a recipe include both milk and lemon or orange juice, the juice should be stirred into the milk very slowly to prevent it from curdling.

The amounts in all the following recipes are for one person.

Hot Apple Juice
(HEISSER APFELSAFT)

Ingredients: 1 glass apple juice, small piece cinnamon, ¾ tsp. lemon juice, sugar, 5 tsp. rum or brandy.

Heat the apple juice with the cinnamon, then remove the latter and pour the juice into a glass with a silver spoon in it (to prevent cracking). Add the lemon juice, a little sugar and finally the brandy or rum. Serve as hot as possible.

Orange Flip
(ORANGEN-FLIP)

Ingredients: Juice of 2 oranges, 1 egg yolk, $\frac{1}{2}$ pt. ($\frac{1}{4}$ l.) milk, $2\frac{1}{2}$ tsp. sugar, $\frac{1}{2}$ tsp. grated orange rind.

Beat the yolk, add the milk and, very slowly, the orange juice. Sweeten, stir vigorously and sprinkle the grated orange rind on top.

Yogurt Flip
(JOGHURT-FLIP)

Ingredients: $\frac{1}{4}$ pt. ($\frac{1}{8}$ l.) yogurt, $2\frac{1}{2}$–5 tsp. sea buckthorn syrup.

Beat the ingredients together and serve at once.

Lemon Juice with Honey
(ZITRONENSAFT MIT HONIG)

Ingredients: 2–3 tsp. honey, juice of $1\frac{1}{2}$ lemons.

Dilute the honey with hot water, add the lemon juice, stir well and serve.

Taken as hot as possible this drink has a soothing effect on chest infections, catarrhal conditions, etc.

Carrot Juice with Lemon
(KAROTTIN-TRUNK)

Ingredients: Juice of 2–3 carrots, juice of 1 lemon, $\frac{1}{3}$ pt. ($\frac{1}{5}$ l.) milk.

Use an electric blender to extract the carrot juice, or grate the carrots finely and squeeze through a hand-operated press. Add the other ingredients and stir well.

Fruit Punch
(OBSTPUNSCH)

Ingredients: $\frac{1}{2}$ pt. ($\frac{1}{4}$ l.) fruit juice (redcurrant, apple or grape), 2 tbsp. sugar, small piece of cinnamon, juice of 1 lemon.

Heat the fruit juice with the sugar and cinnamon, but do not allow to boil. Meanwhile pour the lemon juice into a glass, then add the hot juice, having first removed the cinnamon. A silver spoon in the glass will prevent its cracking.

Sour Milk Pudding with Apples
(SAUERMILCH-APFELSPEISE)

Ingredients: 2 apples, butter, scant ½ pt. (¼ l.) sour milk, 1½–2 tbsp. sugar, 1½–2 tbsp. grated hazelnuts, 1 pkt. (1½ tbsp.) vanilla sugar, 3½ tbsp. grated ryebread or pumpernickel, ¾ tsp. grated lemon rind, 1 egg white.

Peel and slice the apples and place in a small buttered soufflé dish. Mix the hazelnuts and vanilla sugar and scatter over the apples. Beat the sour milk with an egg whisk, add the sugar, grated bread and lemon rind, mix well and pour the mixture over the fruit. Top with the stiffly beaten egg white and bake for 6–10 minutes in a fairly hot oven.

Honey is even better to use than sugar.

Buttermilk with Banana
(BUTTERMILCHBREI MIT BANANEN)

Ingredients: ½ pt. (¼ l.) buttermilk, ½ oz. (15 g.) potato flour, ½–1 banana.

Stir the potato flour into the buttermilk. Bring to the boil, stirring all the time, and allow to simmer for a few moments. Take off the heat and add the mashed banana.

Porridge with Fruit Juice
(PORRIDGE MIT OBSTSAFT)

Ingredients: Scant ½ pt. (¼ l.) milk, pinch of salt, 1 oz. (25 g.) oatmeal, ¼ pt. (⅛ l.) fruit juice or compote or any soft fruit.

Bring the milk, with salt added, to the boil and add the oatmeal. Cook over a low heat until thick, stirring continuously. Tip into a bowl and pour over the fruit juice, or top with drained compote or fresh fruit.

Yogurt with Fruit
(JOGHURT MIT OBST)

Ingredients: ¼ pt. (⅛ l.) yogurt, 3½ oz. (100 g.) soft fruit or 1 banana, 1 egg yolk, 3½–5 tsp. sugar or honey.

Clean the fruit, mash well with a fork and mix the purée with the yogurt. Add the beaten yolk and sweeten with sugar or honey.

Almond Flummery with Fruit
(MANDELFLAMMERI MIT OBST)

Ingredients: Scant ½ pt. (¼ l.) milk, 2½ tsp. sugar, ¾ oz. (20 g.) potato flour, ¾ oz. (20 g.) grated almonds or hazelnuts, 1 egg yolk, scant ½ pt. (¼ l.) purée of soft fruit or compote.

Make a smooth paste with the potato flour and a little milk. Bring the rest of the milk to the boil, add to the paste and allow to simmer for a few moments. Take off the heat and stir in the sugar, beaten yolk and almonds or hazelnuts. Serve decorated with fruit.

Raspberry Cup
(HIMBEER-KALTSCHALE)

Ingredients: 4–5 oz. (125 g.) raspberries, sugar, ½ pt. (¼ l.) milk.

Clean the raspberries and rub about three-quarters of them through a sieve. Sweeten the purée to taste and dilute with the milk. Top with the remaining fruit and serve with sponge biscuits.

Rosehip Soup
(HAGEBUTTENSUPPE)

Ingredients: 4 oz. (125 g.) rosehips, 1½–2 oz. (50 g.) fresh breadcrumbs, 1 egg yolk, sugar, cinnamon.

Clean the rosehips and cook with the breadcrumbs in water until tender. Rub through a sieve and dilute the pulp with a little water if necessary. Bring to the boil once more, take off the heat and stir in the beaten egg yolk. Add sugar and cinnamon to taste.

Add a dash of white wine if alcohol is permitted in the diet.

Stewed Apples with Berries
(GEDÜNSTETE ÄPFEL MIT BEEREN GEFÜLLT)

Ingredients: 2 apples, 3½ tbsp. sugar, 3½ oz. (100 g.) soft fruit
(strawberries, raspberries, redcurrants, bilberries
or blackberries).

Peel and core the apples and carefully poach them in a little
sweetened water. Lift out and fill the opening with fruit. Serve
hot or cold, with or without custard, and hand sponge biscuits or pumpernickel separately.

If fresh fruit is not available, bottled fruit or jam may be
substituted.

Pineapple Soufflé
(ANANAS-AUFLAUF)

Ingredients: 1–2 eggs, ¾ oz. (20 g.) sugar, ¾ tsp. lemon juice,
butter, 3 pineapple rings.

Beat the egg yolks with the sugar very thoroughly, add the
lemon juice, chopped pineapple, and finally the stiffly beaten
egg whites. Pile the mixture into a small, buttered heatproof
dish and bake in an oven set previously at a moderate (350°F
Mark 5) to fairly hot (400°F, Mark 6) temperature for 10–15
minutes. Serve immediately.

Fruit Soufflé
(FRUCHTSCHAUM-AUFLAUF)

Ingredients: 1 pt. (⅝ l.) apple purée or ½ lb. (250 g.) strawberries
or raspberries, 2–3 tbsp. sugar, 2–3 egg whites,
grated lemon rind, butter.

If using raspberries or strawberries, mash with a fork or rub
through a sieve. Sweeten the fruit purée and add grated lemon
rind. Fold in the stiffly beaten egg whites and pile the mixture
into a buttered heatproof dish. Bake in a warm oven for 10
minutes.

A more substantial dish can be prepared by putting a layer
of rice cooked in milk at the bottom of the dish and topping
it with the fruit mixture.

Banana Rice
(REIS-DIÄTSPEISE)

Ingredients: 1–1½ oz. (30–40 g.) pudding rice, pinch of salt, grated lemon rind, milk, 1½–2 tsp. sugar, 1 banana, redcurrant syrup or jelly.

Wash the rice and bring to the boil in salted water. Drain and spray with cold water. Cook in milk, to which grated lemon rind has been added, until very tender. Sweeten to taste, add the mashed banana and serve with redcurrant syrup poured over or decorated with redcurrant jelly.

An alternative suggestion is to cook and sweeten the rice as above, then stir in a well beaten egg yolk and a handful of raisins, previously soaked in water for 1 hour.

Cheese Cream with Orange
(ORANGEN-QUARKCREME)

Ingredients: 8 oz. (250 g.) curd cheese, 1–2 egg yolks, 2–3 tbsp. condensed milk or single cream, juice of 2 oranges, 3½ tbsp. sugar, slices of orange.

Beat the cheese with the milk or cream, egg yolks and orange juice. Sweeten to taste and serve with a garnish of orange slices.

Index

214

215

216

NOTES

NOTES